CLEAN EATING

COOKBOOK UK
FOR BEGINNERS

Eat Better, Feel Better, No-Fuss and
Nutritious Clean Recipes Incl. Whole Foods,
Diabetic Recipes to Fuel Your Life | UK
Measurements & Ingredients

ROBIN SMITH

Table of Contents

INTRODUCTION ·· //1

CHAPTER 1   BREAKFAST ································· //8

CHAPTER 2   GRAIN AND BEANS ····················· //14

CHAPTER 3   BEEF, PORK AND LAMB ··············· //20

CHAPTER 4   VEGETABLES ···························· //26

CHAPTER 5   POULTRY······························· //32

CHAPTER 6   SALAD································· //38

CHAPTER 7   FISH AND SEAFOOD ················ //44

CHAPTER 8   SOUP AND STEWS ·················· //50

CHAPTER 9   APPETIZER AND SIDES ············· //56

CHAPTER 10   SNACK AND DESSERT ·············· //62

APPENDIX 1   30 DAYS MEAL PLAN ·············· //68

APPENDIX 2   BASIC KITCHEN CONVERSIONS & EQUIVALENTS ········ //70

APPENDIX 3   RECIPES INDEX················· //72

INTRODUCTION

Do you ever find yourself caught in the relentless hustle and bustle of modern life, juggling responsibilities, and trying to maintain some semblance of health and well-being? Perhaps you've wrestled with the guilt that can come from indulging in that extra serving of fast food, or the exhaustion that follows an afternoon sugar crash. I know those feelings all too well because I've been there myself.

I used to be just like you — constantly seeking a way to lead a healthier life amid the chaos of daily routines. The never-ending cycle of fad diets and quick-fix solutions left me feeling frustrated and defeated. It wasn't until I stumbled upon a transformative concept that my perspective on food, nutrition, and health underwent a remarkable shift. That concept was clean eating, and it changed my life in ways I could have never imagined.

In this book, I invite you to step on a path toward better health and vitality. Like many, I struggled with maintaining a balanced diet and finding the energy to sustain my busy days. But when I embraced clean eating, everything changed. I found a way to nourish my body that was not only effective but also sustainable and enjoyable.

The Clean Eating Diet, at its core, is about making conscious choices that prioritize wholesome, unprocessed foods while minimizing the consumption of foods laden with artificial additives, refined sugars, and unhealthy fats. It's about embracing foods that are as close to their natural state as possible, preserving their nutritional integrity and benefiting from the abundance of nutrients they offer.

This cookbook is more than just a collection of recipes; it's a guide to adopting a clean eating lifestyle. Inside, you'll find a wealth of delicious and satisfying dishes that prove clean eating doesn't mean sacrificing flavour. From vibrant salads bursting with fresh produce to hearty, nutrient-rich main courses, these recipes are designed to nourish your body and tantalize your taste buds.

As you flip through these pages and walk on your clean eating journey, remember that you are not alone. We're in this together, committed to pursuing vibrant health, increased energy, and a more fulfilling life. Let's begin this transformative journey toward a healthier you, one delicious and nutritious meal at a time.

Introduction to Clean Eating Diet

The Clean Eating, is a dietary regime that has gained widespread popularity in recent years for its focus on eating unprocessed or whole foods while minimizing the intake of highly processed ingredients. This dietary philosophy places a strong emphasis on the quality and source of the foods we eat, prioritizing natural, nutrient-dense choices that support overall health and well-being. At its core, clean eating revolves around the principle that the closer a food is to its natural state, the better it is for our bodies. This means favouring fresh fruits and

Core Principles of Clean Eating

This approach emphasizes on the intake of whole, organic foods which are not processed while minimizing or eliminating highly processed foods. The core principles of clean eating revolve around making healthier food choices to promote overall well-being and support long-term health. Here are the key principles of a clean eating diet:

Whole Foods: Focus on eating whole foods that are as close to their natural state as possible. This includes vegetables, fruits, lean proteins, whole grains, nuts, and seeds.

Minimize Processed Foods: Avoid or limit the intake of processed and highly refined foods such as sugary snacks, sugary drinks, fast food, and heavily processed packaged foods.

Read Labels: When purchasing packaged foods, read ingredient labels carefully. Choose products with minimal ingredients and no added artificial additives, preservatives, or chemicals.

Fresh and Local: Opt for fresh, locally sourced produce and foods whenever possible. This can help you access foods that are in season and often contain more nutrients.

Balance Macronutrients: Strive for a balanced intake of carbohydrates, proteins, and healthy fats. Incorporate a variety of nutrient-dense foods into your meals to ensure you're getting a wide range of essential nutrients.

Portion Control: Be mindful of portion sizes to prevent overeating. Pay attention to hunger and fullness cues, and try to avoid eating large portions of calorie-dense foods.

Hydration: Drink plenty of water throughout the day to stay hydrated. Limit or eliminate sugary beverages and opt for herbal teas, water, or infused water instead.

Limit Added Sugars: Reduce your consumption of foods and beverages high in added sugars, such as soda, candy, and desserts. Choose natural sweeteners like honey or maple syrup in moderation.

Healthy Fats: Include sources of healthy fats in your diet, such as avocados, olive oil, nuts, and fatty fish (like salmon). These fats can support heart health and overall well-being.

Cooking at Home: Cooking your meals at home allows you to have better control over the ingredients and cooking methods used. It also helps you avoid the excessive sodium and unhealthy fats often found in restaurant dishes.

Variety and Moderation: Aim for a varied diet that includes a wide range of foods from different food groups. Moderation is key in clean eating, as it allows you to enjoy occasional treats without feeling deprived.

Remember that clean eating is a flexible approach, and what works for one person may not work for another. It's essential to find a balance that suits your individual preferences, dietary needs, and lifestyle. Additionally, consulting with a healthcare professional or registered dietitian can provide personalized guidance and recommendations to support your clean eating journey.

Benefits of Clean Eating

A clean eating diet, characterized by the consumption of whole, unprocessed foods and the avoidance of highly processed and refined foods, offers numerous potential benefits for your health and well-being. Here are some of the key advantages of following a clean eating diet, explained in detail:

- **Nutrient Density:** Clean eating emphasizes whole foods that are rich in essential nutrients like vitamins, minerals, fibre, and antioxidants. These nutrients are crucial for overall health, supporting bodily functions, boosting the immune system, and reducing the risk of chronic diseases.

- **Weight Management:** Clean eating can be an effective approach for weight management. Whole foods tend to be lower in calories and more filling than processed foods, which can help you control your calorie intake and reduce overeating. Additionally, a diet rich in fibre can promote feelings of fullness, reducing the likelihood of snacking on unhealthy foods.

- **Improved Digestion:** Whole foods, especially fruits, vegetables, and whole grains, are high in dietary fibre. Fiber aids digestion by promoting regular bowel movements and preventing constipation. It also supports a healthy gut microbiome, which is essential for overall digestive health.

- **Steady Energy Levels:** Clean eating promotes stable blood sugar levels because it typically includes complex carbohydrates, healthy fats, and lean proteins. This can help prevent energy crashes and mood swings that often result from consuming sugary and highly processed foods.

- **Heart Health:** A clean eating diet can benefit heart health in several ways. It encourages the consumption of heart-healthy fats like those found in avocados and olive oil, as well as omega-3 fatty acids from sources like fatty fish. Additionally, it reduces the intake of saturated and trans fats commonly found in processed foods, which can lower the risk of heart disease.

- **Lower Risk of Chronic Diseases:** Following a clean eating diet is associated with a reduced risk of chronic diseases such as type 2 diabetes, hypertension, and certain types of cancer. The high intake of antioxidants from fruits and vegetables may help combat oxidative stress and inflammation, two factors contributing to chronic disease development.

- **Improved Skin Health:** Nutrient-rich foods in a clean eating diet, particularly those containing antioxidants and healthy fats, can promote healthier and clearer skin. These foods may help reduce inflammation, fight acne, and slow down the aging process.

- **Enhanced Mental Health:** There is emerging evidence suggesting a link between diet and mental health. Clean eating, with its emphasis on whole, nutrient-dense foods, may support better mood regulation and mental well-being. Omega-3 fatty acids, found in clean eating sources like fatty fish, have also been linked to improved mental health.

- **Better Athletic Performance:** Clean eating provides the body with the necessary nutrients for optimal physical performance and recovery. Whole grains, lean proteins, and nutrient-rich vegetables can help athletes maintain energy levels and support muscle growth and repair.

- **Longevity:** A diet rich in whole foods and low in processed foods is associated with a longer lifespan. Clean eating reduces exposure to additives, preservatives, and artificial ingredients that may have long-term health consequences.

- **Environmental Benefits:** Clean eating often involves choosing locally sourced, sustainably produced foods, which can reduce your carbon footprint and contribute to a more sustainable food system.

While these benefits highlight the advantages of a clean eating diet, it's essential to remember that individual dietary needs and preferences vary. What works best for one person may not work as well for another. Consult with a healthcare professional or registered dietitian to create a personalized dietary plan that aligns with your health goals and needs.

Foods to Include in a Clean Eating Diet

A clean eating diet emphasizes the inclusion of whole, unprocessed foods while minimizing or avoiding highly processed and refined options. Here is a list of foods to include in a clean eating diet:

- **Fruits:** Choose a variety of fresh, frozen, or dried fruits. These provide essential vitamins, minerals, fibre, and antioxidants. Examples include berries, apples, oranges, bananas, and pears.

- **Vegetables:** Incorporate a colourful array of vegetables in your diet. Opt for fresh, frozen, or canned (with no added salt or sugar) options. Leafy greens, broccoli, carrots, bell peppers, and sweet potatoes are excellent choices.

- **Whole Grains:** Choose whole grains over refined grains. These grains are higher in fibre and nutrients. Examples include brown rice, quinoa, oats, whole wheat pasta, and whole-grain bread.

- **Lean Proteins:** Include sources of lean protein in your diet to support muscle health and overall satiety. Good options include skinless poultry, lean cuts of beef or pork, tofu, tempeh, legumes (beans, lentils, chickpeas), and fish (especially fatty fish like salmon and mackerel).

Healthy Fats: Incorporate sources of healthy fats, which are important for heart health and overall well-being. These include avocados, nuts (e.g., almonds, walnuts), seeds (e.g., chia seeds, flaxseeds), olive oil, and fatty fish.

- **Dairy or Dairy Alternatives:** Choose low-fat or non-fat dairy products, or dairy alternatives like almond milk, coconut yogurt, or soy-based products. Be mindful of added sugars in some dairy alternatives.

- **Herbs and Spices:** Use herbs and spices to flavour your dishes instead of relying on salt or high-sodium seasonings. Fresh herbs like basil, cilantro, and thyme, as well as spices like turmeric, cumin, and cinnamon, can enhance the taste of your meals.

- **Legumes:** Legumes are an excellent source of plant-based protein and fibre. Include beans (e.g., black beans, kidney beans), lentils, and chickpeas in soups, salads, or as a meat substitute in various recipes.

- **Nuts and Seeds:** These provide healthy fats, protein, and a variety of vitamins and minerals. Enjoy them as a snack or sprinkle them on salads, yogurt, or oatmeal.

- **Eggs:** Eggs are a nutritious source of protein, vitamins, and minerals. They can be prepared in various ways, such as boiled, scrambled, or as an omelette.

- **Natural Sweeteners:** If you need to sweeten your food or beverages, opt for natural sweeteners like honey or maple syrup in moderation. Avoid artificial sweeteners and excessive added sugars.

- **Water:** Staying well-hydrated is essential for overall health. Drink plenty of water throughout the day and consider herbal teas or infused water for variety.

- **Tea and Coffee:** Unsweetened tea and black coffee (in moderation) can be part of a clean eating diet, as they are low in calories and can provide antioxidants.

- **Fatty Fish:** Fatty fish like salmon, mackerel, and sardines are rich in omega-3 fatty acids, which support heart and brain health.

- **Unsweetened Yogurt:** Choose plain, unsweetened yogurt or Greek yogurt for a source of probiotics and protein. Add your own fresh fruit or a drizzle of honey for sweetness.

Tailor your clean eating plan to your individual dietary preferences and needs, and consider consulting with a registered dietitian for personalized guidance.

Foods to Avoid or Minimize

In a clean eating diet, the goal is to minimize or entirely avoid highly processed, refined, and unhealthy foods that can contribute to poor health and well-being. Here's a list of foods to avoid or minimize:

- **Processed and Sugary Snacks:** These often contain high levels of added sugars, unhealthy fats, and artificial additives. Examples include chips, candy, cookies, pastries, and sugary cereals.

- **Sugary Beverages:** Beverages like soda, energy drinks, fruit juices with added sugars, and sugary coffee drinks can contribute to weight gain and are typically low in nutrients.

- **Fast Food:** Fast food items are usually high in unhealthy fats, sodium, and calories. Burgers, fries, fried chicken, and other fast-food items should be minimized or avoided.

- **White Bread and Refined Grains:** Replace white bread and other refined grain products (white rice, regular pasta) with whole grains. Refined grains have had their fibre and nutrients stripped away.

- **Processed Meats:** Reduce consumption of processed meats like hot dogs, sausages, bacon, and deli meats, which can be high in sodium and preservatives. Opt for lean, unprocessed meats or plant-based protein sources.

- **Highly Processed Convenience Foods:** Avoid packaged convenience foods such as frozen meals, microwaveable dinners, and pre-packaged snacks. These often contain hidden sugars, unhealthy fats, and high levels of sodium.

- **Canned Soups and Sauces with Added Sodium:** Canned soups, sauces, and other canned goods can be high in sodium. Look for low-sodium or no-salt-added options, or prepare your own soups and sauces from scratch.

- **Sweets and Desserts:** Limit or eliminate desserts like ice cream, cakes, and pies that are loaded with added sugars and unhealthy fats. Consider healthier dessert options made with whole ingredients.

- **Processed Condiments:** Some condiments like ketchup, salad dressings, and barbecue sauce can contain added sugars and unhealthy fats. Choose condiments with minimal additives or make your own.

- **Artificial Sweeteners:** Avoid artificial sweeteners like aspartame and saccharin, which are often found in diet sodas and sugar-free products. They may have negative health effects.

- **Highly Processed Cooking Oils:** Replace highly refined and processed cooking oils (e.g., vegetable oil, soybean oil) with healthier options like olive oil, avocado oil, or coconut oil.

- **Excessive Salt:** Minimize your intake of foods with high salt content, such as salty snacks, canned soups, and processed meats. Excess sodium can contribute to hypertension and other health issues.

- **Alcohol:** While moderate alcohol consumption may be acceptable for some, it's essential to consume alcohol in moderation or avoid it altogether. Excessive alcohol intake can have negative health effects.

- **Artificial Additives and Preservatives:** Be cautious of foods with long ingredient lists full of artificial additives, preservatives, and artificial colours. These are often found in heavily processed foods.

- **Trans Fats:** Stay away from foods containing trans fats, as they are linked to heart disease. Check ingredient labels for hydrogenated or partially hydrogenated oils.

The key is to focus on nutrient-dense options and minimize your exposure to highly processed and unhealthy ingredients.

Challenges to Overcome

The Clean Eating Diet, while undeniably beneficial for health, can present its fair share of challenges. One common hurdle is the convenience of highly processed and fast-food options, which often seem like time-savers in our hectic lives. Another challenge lies in the social aspect of eating, as clean eating choices may differ from those of friends and family, potentially leading to feelings of isolation or resistance to change. The misconception that clean eating is expensive can be discouraging. To overcome these challenges, it's essential to plan ahead, prioritize meal preparation, and build a support network of like-minded individuals. Additionally, educate yourself about affordable clean eating options, explore new recipes to keep your meals exciting, and remember that the long-term benefits of improved health and vitality far outweigh any temporary convenience or social pressures.

Transitioning to a Clean Eating Diet

Transitioning to a clean eating diet can be a positive step toward improving your overall health and well-being. Here are some tips to help you make a successful transition:

- **Start Gradually:** Instead of making drastic changes overnight, ease into clean eating. Gradual changes are more sustainable and can help you adapt to new eating habits.

- **Educate Yourself:** Learn about the principles of clean eating and the benefits it offers. Understanding why you're making these changes can motivate you to stick with them.

- **Plan Your Meals:** Create a meal plan for the week that includes clean eating recipes and a shopping list. Planning ahead can prevent last-minute unhealthy food choices.

- **Clean Out Your Kitchen:** Go through your pantry and refrigerator to remove processed and unhealthy foods. Replace them with whole, clean options.

- **Cook at Home:** Preparing your meals at home gives you control over the ingredients and cooking methods. Experiment with clean eating recipes to discover new flavours.

- **Embrace Whole Foods:** Prioritize whole foods like fruits, vegetables, lean proteins, whole grains, nuts, and seeds. These should form the foundation of your clean eating diet.

- **Snack Wisely:** Choose healthy snacks like fresh fruit, veggies with hummus, Greek yogurt, or nuts. Having nutritious snacks on hand can prevent you from reaching for processed options.

- **Avoid Liquid Calories:** Cut back on sugary drinks and alcohol, as they can contribute empty calories. Opt for water, herbal teas, or infused water instead.

- **Include Protein:** Incorporate lean protein sources into your meals to help you feel full and satisfied. Examples include chicken, fish, beans, and tofu.

- **Experiment with Herbs and Spices:** Use herbs and spices to add flavour to your dishes without relying on excessive salt or high-sugar sauces and seasonings.

- **Treat Yourself in Moderation:** While clean eating is about making nutritious choices, it's okay to enjoy an occasional treat. The key is moderation.

- **Stay Flexible:** Don't be too hard on yourself if you occasionally stray from your clean eating plan. It's normal to have occasional indulgences; what matters is your overall pattern of eating.

CHAPTER 1
BREAKFAST

Cinnamon Apple French Toast Bake / 9

Kale and Quinoa Egg Casserole / 9

Apple-Cranberry Quinoa / 10

Savoury Spinach Oatmeal / 10

Mixed Nuts Berry Granola / 11

Baked Berries Oatmeal / 11

Garlic Root Vegetable Hash / 12

Grain Granola with Dry Cherries / 12

Spicy Eggs in Purgatory / 12

Potato, Tomato and Egg Strata / 13

Mediterranean Spinach Strata / 13

Cinnamon Apple French Toast Bake

SERVES 8

| PREP TIME: 14 minutes
| COOK TIME: 5 hours

8 eggs
10 slices whole-wheat bread, cubed
2 Granny Smith apples, peeled and diced
1 cup granola
240ml canned unsweetened coconut milk
240ml unsweetened apple juice
120ml coconut sugar
2 tsps. vanilla extract
1 tsp. ground cinnamon
¼ tsp. ground cardamom

1. Grease a 5.5 litre slow cooker lightly with plain vegetable oil.
2. Mix the coconut sugar, cinnamon, and cardamom in a small bowl.
3. Layer the bread, apples, and coconut sugar mixture in the slow cooker.
4. Mix the eggs, coconut milk, apple juice, and vanilla in a large bowl, and mix well. Add this mixture slowly over the food in the slow cooker. Scatter the granola on top.
5. Cover the slow cooker and cook on low for 4 to 5 hours, or until a food thermometer registers 75°C.
6. Ladle the mixture from the slow cooker to serve.

Nutritional Info per Serving
calories: 317, fat: 9g, protein: 12g, carbs: 49g, fibre: 6g, sugar: 18g, sodium: 326mg

Kale and Quinoa Egg Casserole

SERVES 6-8

| PREP TIME: 13 minutes
| COOK TIME: 8 hours

11 eggs
3 cups chopped kale
700ml 2% milk
90g quinoa, rinsed and drained
340g shredded low-fat Havarti cheese
340ml low-sodium vegetable broth
1 leek, chopped
1 red bell pepper, stemmed, seeded, and chopped
3 garlic cloves, minced

1. Grease a 5.5 litre slow cooker lightly with vegetable oil and keep aside.
2. Mix the milk, vegetable broth, and eggs in a large bowl, and beat well with a wire whisk.
3. Stir in the kale, quinoa, leek, bell pepper, garlic, and cheese. Add this mixture into the prepared slow cooker.
4. Cover the slow cooker and cook on low for 6 to 8 hours, or until a food thermometer registers 75°C and the mixture is set. Serve warm.

Nutritional Info per Serving
calories: 483, fat: 27g, protein: 25g, carbs: 32g, fibre: 3g, sugar: 8g, sodium: 462mg

Apple-Cranberry Quinoa

SERVES 12

| PREP TIME: 12 minutes
| COOK TIME: 8 hours

540g quinoa, rinsed and drained
950ml canned unsweetened coconut milk
470ml unsweetened apple juice
340g dried cranberries
470ml water
85g honey
30g walnut
1 tsp. ground cinnamon
1 tsp. vanilla extract
½ tsp. salt

1. Mix all the ingredients in a 5.5 litre slow cooker. Cover the slow cooker and cook on low for 6 to 8 hours or until the quinoa is creamy. Serve warm.

Nutritional Info per Serving

calories: 284, fat: 4g, protein: 6g, carbs: 55g, fibre: 4g, sugar: 25g, sodium: 104mg

Savoury Spinach Oatmeal

SERVES 6-8

| PREP TIME: 12 minutes
| COOK TIME: 8 hours

270g steel-cut oatmeal
60g chopped baby spinach leaves
60g grated low-fat Parmesan cheese
60g mushroom
1.2l low-sodium vegetable broth
240ml water
2 shallots, peeled and minced
2 tbsps. chopped fresh basil
1 tsp. dried basil leaves
1 egg
½ tsp. dried thyme leaves
¼ tsp. salt
¼ tsp. freshly ground black pepper

1. Mix the oatmeal, shallots, vegetable broth, water, basil, thyme, salt, and pepper in a 5.5 litre slow cooker. Cover the slow cooker and cook on low for 7 to 8 hours, or until the oatmeal is soft.
2. Stir in the spinach, Parmesan cheese, mushroom, egg and basil, and allow to stand, covered, for another 5 minutes. Stir and serve warm.

Nutritional Info per Serving

calories: 262, fat: 5g, protein: 8g, carbs: 43g, fibre: 6g, sugar: 2g, sodium: 172mg

Mixed Nuts Berry Granola

SERVES 20 CUPS

| PREP TIME: 11 minutes
| COOK TIME: 5 hours

900g rolled oats
300g whole walnuts
300g whole almonds
300g macadamia nuts
260g dried blueberries
260g dried cherries
170g honey
1 tbsp. vanilla extract
2 tsps. ground cinnamon
¼ tsp. ground cardamom

1. Mix the oatmeal, almonds, walnuts, and macadamia nuts in a 5.5 litre slow cooker.
2. Mix the honey, cinnamon, cardamom, and vanilla in a small bowl. Pour this mixture over the oatmeal mixture in the slow cooker and stir with a spatula to coat well.
3. Partially cover the slow cooker. Cook on low for 3½ to 5 hours, stirring twice during the cooking time, until the oatmeal and nuts are completely toasted.
4. Transfer the granola from the slow cooker and lay on two large baking sheets. Place the dried blueberries and cherries to the granola and stir carefully.
5. Allow the granola to cool and serve.

Nutritional Info per Serving

calories: 255, fat: 12g, protein: 6g, carbs: 33g, fibre: 4g, sugar: 16g, sodium: 14mg

Baked Berries Oatmeal

SERVES 14

| PREP TIME: 10 minutes
| COOK TIME: 6 hours

2 tbsps. melted coconut oil
630g rolled oats
340g dried blueberries
200g dried cherries
4 eggs
340ml unsweetened almond milk
110g honey
1 tsp. ground cinnamon
¼ tsp. ground ginger
¼ tsp. salt

1. Grease a 5.5 litre slow cooker lightly with plain vegetable oil.
2. Add the rolled oats in a large bowl.
3. Mix the eggs, almond milk, coconut oil, honey, salt, cinnamon, and ginger in a medium bowl. Mix until combined well. Add this mixture over the oats.
4. Slowly stir in the dried blueberries and dried cherries. Pour into the prepared slow cooker.
5. Cover the slow cooker and cook on low for 4 to 6 hours, or until the oatmeal mixture is set and the edges start to brown. Enjoy!

Nutritional Info per Serving

calories: 368, fat: 7g, protein: 9g, carbs: 68g, fibre: 6g, sugar: 33g, sodium: 97mg

Garlic Root Vegetable Hash

SERVES 8

| PREP TIME: 18 minutes
| COOK TIME: 8 hours

2 tbsps. olive oil	2 onions, chopped
4 Yukon Gold potatoes, chopped	2 garlic cloves, minced
3 large carrots, peeled and chopped	60ml vegetable broth
2 russet potatoes, chopped	1 tsp. dried thyme leaves
1 large parsnip, peeled and chopped	½ tsp. salt

1. Mix all the ingredients in a 5.5 litre slow cooker. Cover the slow cooker and cook on low for 7 to 8 hours.
2. Stir the hash well and serve warm.

Nutritional Info per Serving

calories: 150, fat: 4g, protein: 3g, carbs: 28g, fibre: 4g, sugar: 4g, sodium: 176mg

Grain Granola with Dry Cherries

SERVES 40

| PREP TIME: 12 minutes
| COOK TIME: 5 hours

450g regular oatmeal	400g golden raisins
800g barley flakes	260g dried cherries
150g buckwheat flakes	170g honey
300g whole walnuts	2 tsps. ground cinnamon
300g whole almonds	1 tbsp. vanilla extract

1. Mix the oatmeal, barley flakes, buckwheat flakes, almonds, and walnuts in a 5.5 litre slow cooker.
2. Mix the honey, cinnamon, and vanilla in a small bowl, and combine well. Pour this mixture over the food in the slow cooker and stir with a spatula to coat well.
3. Partially cover the slow cooker. Cook on low for 3½ to 5 hours, stirring twice during the cooking time, until the oatmeal, barley and buckwheat flakes, and nuts are completely toasted.
4. Remove the granola from the slow cooker and lay on two large baking sheets. Place the raisins and cherries to the granola and stir slowly.
5. Allow the granola to cool and serve immediately.

Nutritional Info per Serving

calories: 214, fat: 8g, protein: 6g, carbs: 33g, fibre: 4g, sugar: 13g, sodium: 17mg

Spicy Eggs in Purgatory

SERVES 10

| PREP TIME: 14 minutes
| COOK TIME: 8 hours

1.1 kg Roma tomatoes, chopped	2 garlic cloves, chopped
8 large eggs	15g chopped flat-leaf parsley
240ml low-sodium vegetable broth	1 tsp. paprika
2 onions, chopped	½ tsp. ground cumin
2 red chilli peppers, minced	½ tsp. dried marjoram leaves

1. Mix the tomatoes, onions, garlic, paprika, cumin, marjoram, and vegetable broth in a 5.5 litre slow cooker, and stir to mix well. Cover the slow cooker and cook on low for 7 to 8 hours, or until a sauce has formed.
2. One at a time, gently break the eggs into the sauce; do not stir.
3. Cover and cook on high until the egg whites are fully set and the yolk is thickened, for about 20 minutes. Scatter the eggs with the minced red chilli peppers.
4. Garnish with the parsley and serve warm.

Nutritional Info per Serving

calories: 116, fat: 5g, protein: 8g, carbs: 10g, fibre: 2g, sugar: 5g, sodium: 112mg

Potato, Tomato and Egg Strata

SERVES 10-12

| PREP TIME: 18 minutes
| COOK TIME: 8 hours

8 eggs
8 Yukon Gold potatoes, peeled and diced
3 Roma tomatoes, seeded and chopped
340 g shredded low-fat Swiss cheese
2 red bell peppers, stemmed, seeded, and minced
240 ml 2% milk
2 egg whites
1 onion, minced
3 garlic cloves, minced
1 tsp. dried marjoram leaves

1. Lay the diced potatoes, onion, bell peppers, tomatoes, garlic, and cheese in a 5.5 litre slow cooker.
2. Mix the eggs, egg whites, marjoram, and milk well with a wire whisk in a medium bowl. Add this mixture into the slow cooker.
3. Cover the slow cooker and cook on low for 6 to 8 hours, or until a food thermometer registers 75°C and the potatoes are soft.
4. Scoop the strata out of the slow cooker to serve.

Nutritional Info per Serving

calories: 305, fat: 12g, protein: 17g, carbs: 33g, fibre: 3g, sugar: 5g, sodium: 136mg

Mediterranean Spinach Strata

SERVES 10-12

| PREP TIME: 16 minutes
| COOK TIME: 7 hours

2 tbsps. olive oil
10 slices whole-wheat bread, cut into cubes
60g chopped baby spinach leaves
4 eggs
2 egg whites
340ml 2% milk
120g shredded low-fat Asiago cheese
2 red bell peppers, stemmed, seeded, and chopped
1 onion, finely chopped
3 garlic cloves, minced

1. Mix the bread cubes, onion, garlic, bell peppers, and spinach in a 5.5 litre slow cooker.
2. Mix the eggs, egg whites, olive oil, and milk in a medium bowl, and beat well. Add this mixture into the slow cooker. Sprinkle with the cheese.
3. Cover the slow cooker and cook on low for 5 to 7 hours, or until a food thermometer registers 75°C and the strata is set and puffed.
4. Ladle the strata out of the slow cooker to serve.

Nutritional Info per Serving

calories: 385, fat: 11g, protein: 16g, carbs: 55g, fibre: 8g, sugar: 11g, sodium: 572mg

CHAPTER 2

GRAIN AND BEANS

Wild Rice with Parsley / 15

Roasted Beet, Kale and Quinoa / 15

Barley Risotto with Mushroom / 16

Garlic Barley and Black Beans / 16

Rosemary White Beans with Onion / 17

Herbed Succotash with Tomato / 17

Cheesy Risotto with Green Beans and

Sweet Potatoes / 18

Quinoa with Mushroom and Carrot / 18

Thai Green Bean and Soybean / 18

Vegetables and Grains / 19

Garlicky Tofu and Brussels Sprouts / 19

Wild Rice with Parsley

SERVES 8

| PREP TIME: 5 minutes
| COOK TIME: 6 hours

600g wild rice, rinsed and drained
1.5l low-sodium vegetable broth
1 onion, chopped
20g chopped fresh flat-leaf parsley
1 bay leaf
½ tsp. dried thyme leaves
½ tsp. dried basil leaves
½ tsp. salt

1. Mix the wild rice, vegetable broth, onion, salt, thyme, basil, and bay leaf in a 5.5 litre slow cooker. Cover the slow cooker and cook on low for 4 to 6 hours, or until the wild rice is tender but still firm. You can cook this longer until the wild rice pops that will take about 7 to 8 hours.
2. Remove the bay leaf and discard.
3. Toss in the parsley and serve warm.

Nutritional Info per Serving

calories: 258, fat: 2g, protein: 6g, carbs: 54g, fibre: 5g, sugar: 3g, sodium: 257mg

Roasted Beet, Kale and Quinoa

SERVES 2

| PREP TIME: 4 minutes
| COOK TIME: 55 minutes

1 tbsp. coconut oil
2 tbsps. extra-virgin olive oil
4 baby beetroot, scrubbed, peeled, and halved
70g kale, chopped
90g cup red quinoa, rinsed and drained
2 garlic cloves, minced
240ml water

2 tbsps. freshly squeezed orange juice
1½ tsps. raw honey
1 tsp. tamari
½ tsp. balsamic vinegar
Sea salt
Freshly ground black pepper

1. Preheat the oven to 180°C.
2. On a baking sheet, arrange the halved beetroot and drizzle the coconut oil over the top. Sprinkle with salt and pepper. Roast the beetroot for about 30 to 35 minutes, or until they are fork-tender. Let them cool for at least 5 minutes.
3. When the beetroot are roasting, bring the quinoa and water to a boil over high heat in a large pot, stirring constantly. Turn the heat to low and simmer for about 15 to 20 minutes, stirring occasionally. Once the liquid is absorbed and the quinoa is tender, take the pot from the heat.
4. Combine the beetroot, quinoa, and the kale in a large mixing bowl, and mix well. Divide this equally between 2 serving bowls.
5. Whisk together the olive oil, orange juice, garlic, honey, tamari, and balsamic vinegar in a small bowl. Drizzle the dressing over the quinoa, beet, and kale mixture, and serve immediately.

Nutritional Info per Serving

calories: 447, fat: 23g, protein: 11g, carbs: 52g, fibre: 9g, sugar: 17g, sodium: 385mg

Barley Risotto with Mushroom

SERVES 6-8

| PREP TIME: 12 minutes
| COOK TIME: 8 hours

227 g package button mushrooms, chopped
200 g hulled barley, rinsed
1.5 l low-sodium vegetable broth
55 g grated low-fat Parmesan cheese
1 onion, finely chopped
4 garlic cloves, minced
½ tsp. dried marjoram leaves
⅛ tsp. freshly ground black pepper

1. Mix the barley, onion, garlic, mushrooms, broth, marjoram, and pepper in a 5.5 litre slow cooker. Cover with lid and cook on low for 7 to 8 hours, or until the barley has absorbed most of the liquid and is soft, and the vegetables are tender.
2. Toss in the Parmesan cheese and serve warm.

Nutritional Info per Serving
calories: 288, fat: 6g, protein: 13g, carbs: 45g, fibre: 9g, sugar: 6g, sodium: 495mg

Garlic Barley and Black Beans

SERVES 10

| PREP TIME: 7 minutes
| COOK TIME: 8 hours

340g hulled barley
260g dried black beans, rinsed and drained
2l low-sodium vegetable broth
1 onion, chopped
3 garlic cloves, minced
1 bay leaf
½ tsp. dried thyme leaves

1. Mix all the ingredients in a 5.5 litre slow cooker. Cover and cook on low for 7 to 8 hours, or until the barley and black beans are soft.
2. Remove the bay leaf and discard. Serve warm.

Nutritional Info per Serving
calories: 240, fat: 1g, protein: 12g, carbs: 46g, fibre: 14g, sugar: 2g, sodium: 115mg

Rosemary White Beans with Onion

SERVES 16

| PREP TIME: 8 minutes
| COOK TIME: 8 hours

454 g great northern beans
470ml low sodium vegetable broth
950ml water
1 onion, finely chopped
3 cloves garlic, minced
1 large sprig fresh rosemary
½ tsp. salt
⅛ tsp. white pepper

1. Sort over the beans, remove and discard any extraneous material. Rinse the beans well over cold water and drain.
2. In a 5.5 litre slow cooker, combine the beans, onion, garlic, rosemary, salt, water, and vegetable broth.
3. Cover the slow cooker and cook on low for 6 to 8 hours or until the beans are soft.
4. Remove and discard the rosemary stem. Stir in the mixture gently and serve warm.

Nutritional Info per Serving

calories: 88, fat: 0g, protein: 5g, carbs: 17g, fibre: 5g, sugar: 0g, sodium: 362mg

Herbed Succotash with Tomato

SERVES 10

| PREP TIME: 14 minutes
| COOK TIME: 9 hours

700g frozen corn
360g dry lima beans, rinsed and drained
4 large tomatoes, seeded and chopped
1.2l low-sodium vegetable broth
1 red onion, minced
1 bay leaf
1 tsp. dried thyme leaves
1 tsp. dried basil leaves

1. Mix all the ingredients in a 5.5 litre slow cooker. Cover the slow cooker and cook on low for 8 to 9 hours, or until the lima beans are soft. Remove the bay leaf and discard. Serve warm.

Nutritional Info per Serving

calories: 128, fat: 1g, protein: 6g, carbs: 27g, fibre: 6g, sugar: 10g, sodium: 73mg

Cheesy Risotto with Green Beans and Sweet Potatoes

SERVES 8-10

| PREP TIME: 10 minutes
| COOK TIME: 5 hours

3 tbsps. almond butter
400g short-grain brown rice
1 large sweet potato, peeled and chopped
360g green beans, cut in half crosswise
360g frozen baby peas

1.7l low-sodium vegetable broth
60g grated low-fat Parmesan cheese
1 onion, chopped
5 garlic cloves, minced
1 tsp. dried thyme leaves

1. Mix the sweet potato, onion, garlic, rice, thyme, and broth in a 5.5 litre slow cooker. Cover the slow cooker and cook on low for 3 to 4 hours, or until the rice is tender.
2. Toss in the green beans and frozen peas. Cover and cook on low for about 30 to 40 minutes or until the vegetables are soft.
3. Stir in the cheese and almond butter. Cover and cook on low for 20 minutes, then toss and serve warm.

Nutritional Info per Serving

calories: 385, fat: 10g, protein: 10g, carbs: 52g, fibre: 6g, sugar: 10g, sodium: 426mg

Quinoa with Mushroom and Carrot

SERVES 8-10

| PREP TIME: 8 minutes
| COOK TIME: 6 hours

360g quinoa, rinsed and drained
950ml low-sodium vegetable broth
90g sliced cremini mushrooms
2 carrots, peeled and sliced
2 onions, chopped

3 garlic cloves, minced
1 tsp. dried marjoram leaves
½ tsp. salt
⅛ tsp. freshly ground black pepper

1. Mix all of the ingredients in a 5.5 litre slow cooker. Cover the slow cooker and cook on low for 5 to 6 hours, or until the quinoa and vegetables are soft.
2. Stir in the mixture and serve warm.

Nutritional Info per Serving

calories: 204, fat: 3g, protein: 7g, carbs: 35g, fibre: 4g, sugar: 4g, sodium: 229mg

Thai Green Bean and Soybean

SERVES 8-10

| PREP TIME: 86 minutes
| COOK TIME: 3½ hours

680 g green beans
540g fresh soybeans
3 bulbs fennel, cored and chopped
1 jalapeño pepper, minced
120ml canned unsweetened coconut milk
20g chopped fresh coriander
1 lemongrass stalk
2 tbsps. lime juice
½ tsp. salt

1. Mix the green beans, soybeans, fennel, jalapeño pepper, lemongrass, coconut milk, lime juice, and salt in a 5.5 litre slow cooker. Cover the slow cooker and cook on low for 3 to 3½ hours, or until the vegetables are soft.
2. Remove the lemongrass and discard. Scatter the vegetables with the coriander and serve warm.

Nutritional Info per Serving

calories: 115, fat: 5g, protein: 6g, carbs: 11g, fibre: 6g, sugar: 4g, sodium: 154mg

Vegetables and Grains

SERVES 2

| PREP TIME: 6 minutes
| COOK TIME: 20 minutes

1½ tbsps. extra-virgin olive oil
70g kale, chopped
175g broccoli florets
175g chopped Brussels sprouts
75g roughly chopped carrots
75g red quinoa, rinsed and drained
40g almonds
5g chopped fresh parsley

240ml water
Juice of 1 lemon
1 tbsp. sunflower seeds
½ tbsp. Dijon mustard
1 tsp. organic maple syrup
Sea salt
Freshly ground black pepper

1. In a large pot, bring the quinoa and water to a boil over high heat, stirring constantly. Turn the heat to low and simmer for about 15 to 20 minutes, stirring occasionally. Once the liquid is absorbed and the quinoa is soft, take the pot from the heat.
2. When the quinoa is cooking, combine the broccoli florets, Brussels sprouts, kale, carrots, parsley, almonds, and sunflower seeds in a food processor. Pulse until the veggies are roughly chopped.
3. Whisk together the olive oil, mustard, maple syrup, lemon juice, salt, and pepper until well combined in a small bowl.
4. Fluff the quinoa with a fork and evenly divide it between 2 bowls. Top the quinoa with the salad mixture and pour the dressing over the top. Stir to mix or leave separated. Enjoy!

Nutritional Info per Serving
calories: 281, fat: 10g, protein: 10g, carbs: 41g, fibre: 7g, sugar: 5g, sodium: 260mg

Garlicky Tofu and Brussels Sprouts

SERVES 4

| PREP TIME: 18 minutes
| COOK TIME: 30 minutes

Nonstick cooking spray
397 g package extra-firm organic tofu, drained and cut into 2.5cm pieces
2 tbsps. balsamic vinegar
1 tbsp. extra-virgin olive oil plus 1 tsp.
1 tbsp. garlic, minced
¼ tsp. salt
¼ tsp. black pepper, freshly ground
454 g Brussels sprouts, quartered
95g dried cherries
30g roasted salted pumpkin seeds
1 tbsp. balsamic glaze

1. Preheat the oven to 205°C. Line a large baking sheet with foil and coat it with cooking spray.
2. Place the tofu pieces between 2 clean towels. Rest for 15 minutes to wick away additional liquid.
3. In a large bowl, whisk the vinegar, 1 tbsp. of oil, the garlic, salt, and pepper. Add the tofu and Brussels sprouts and toss gently. Transfer the ingredients to the baking sheet and evenly spread into a layer. Roast for 20 minutes.
4. Remove from the oven and toss its contents. Sprinkle the cherries and pumpkin seeds on top of the Brussels sprouts and tofu. Return to the oven and roast for an additional 10 minutes. Remove from the oven and drizzle with balsamic glaze. Toss to coat.
5. Evenly portion into 4 large glass meal-prep containers with lids. Cover and refrigerate.

Nutritional Info per Serving
calories: 296, fat: 11g, protein: 16g, carbs: 34g, fibre: 8g, sugar: 18g, sodium: 197mg

CHAPTER 3

BEEF, PORK AND LAMB

Sweet Pepper with Sirloin / 21

Moroccan Beef Tagine / 21

Mustard Beef Brisket / 22

Pork Chops and Carrot / 22

BBQ Pulled Pork / 23

Apples-Onions Pork Chops / 23

Classic Moroccan Beef in Lettuce Cups / 24

Classic Lamb and Aubergine Tikka Masala / 24

Feta Lamb Burgers / 24

Beef and Mushroom Lo Mein / 25

Beef Tenderloin with Onion Marmalade / 25

Sweet Pepper with Sirloin

SERVES 4

| PREP TIME: 12 minutes
| COOK TIME: 20 minutes

454 g boneless top sirloin steak, about 2.5cm thick, trimmed of visible fat
1 tbsp. olive oil, plus more for brushing the steak
Salt and freshly ground black pepper
1 small red onion, peeled and thinly sliced
2 tsps. garlic, minced
2 yellow bell peppers, seeded and thinly sliced
2 red bell peppers, seeded and thinly sliced
1 orange bell pepper, seeded and thinly sliced
225g baby spinach
250g halved cherry tomatoes
150g crumbled low-fat blue cheese

1. Preheat a barbecue or oven to medium-high heat.
2. Brush the steak on both sides with the olive oil and season with salt and pepper to taste.
3. Grill the steak, flipping once, until it reaches the desired doneness, about 5 minutes per side for medium 70°C. Or in the oven, broil the steak, turning once. For medium, broil the meat 6 minutes per side or until a meat thermometer reads 70°C.
4. Transfer the steak to a cutting board and slice it against the grain into slices.
5. In a large frying pan on the stove, heat the remaining tbsp. of oil over medium heat and sauté the onion and garlic until softened, 3 minutes.
6. Add the peppers and sauté until tender but still crisp, about 5 minutes.
7. Add the spinach and cherry tomatoes. Stir until the spinach is wilted, about 2 minutes.
8. Season with pepper to taste. Divide peppers among 4 plates and top with about 4 steak pieces each and a sprinkle of blue cheese.

Nutritional Info per Serving

calories: 364, fat: 16g, protein: 40g, carbs: 13g, fibre: 2g, sugar: 8g, sodium: 13mg

Moroccan Beef Tagine

SERVES 8-10

| PREP TIME: 15 minutes
| COOK TIME: 10 hours

1.4 kg grass-fed beef sirloin roast, cut into 5cm pieces
3 carrots, cut into chunks
300g chopped pumpkin
225g chopped dates
2 jalapeño peppers, minced
2 onions, chopped
240ml low-sodium beef stock
6 garlic cloves, minced
2 tbsps. honey
2 tsps. ground cumin
1 tsp. ground turmeric

1. Mix the onions, garlic, jalapeño peppers, carrots, pumpkin and dates in a 5.5 litre slow cooker. Place the beef on top.
2. In a small bowl, mix the beef stock, honey, cumin, and turmeric until combined well. Pour the mixture into the slow cooker.
3. Cover the slow cooker and cook on low for 8 to 10 hours, or until the beef is soft. Enjoy!

Nutritional Info per Serving

calories: 452, fat: 21g, protein: 35g, carbs: 29g, fibre: 4g, sugar: 22g, sodium: 154mg

Mustard Beef Brisket

SERVES 12

| PREP TIME: 15 minutes
| COOK TIME: 11 hours

1.4 kg grass-fed beef brisket, trimmed
227 g BPA-free cans no-salt-added tomato sauce
80g natural mustard
3 onions, chopped
8 garlic cloves, minced
3 tbsps. honey
2 tsps. paprika
1 tsp. dried marjoram leaves
1 tsp. dried oregano leaves
½ tsp. cayenne pepper

1. Mix the onions and garlic in a 5.5 litre slow cooker.
2. In a small bowl, mix the oregano, marjoram, paprika, and cayenne. Gently rub this mixture into the beef brisket.
3. Mix the tomato sauce, mustard, and honey until well combined in another small bowl.
4. Place the beef on the onions and garlic in the slow cooker. Add the tomato mixture over all.
5. Cover the slow cooker and cook on low for 8 to 11 hours, or until the beef is very soft.
6. Slice or shred the beef and serve it on buns.

Nutritional Info per Serving

calories: 303, fat: 10g, protein: 37g, carbs: 18g, fibre: 2g, sugar: 12g, sodium: 277mg

Pork Chops and Carrot

SERVES 8

| PREP TIME: 20 minutes
| COOK TIME: 8 hours

142 g pork chops
4 large carrots, peeled and cut into chunks
120ml low-sodium chicken stock
2 onions, chopped
3 garlic cloves, minced
3 tbsps. grated fresh ginger root
3 tbsps. honey
½ tsp. ground ginger
½ tsp. salt
⅛ tsp. freshly ground black pepper

1. Mix the onions, garlic, and carrots in a 5.5 litre slow cooker. Place the pork chops on top.
2. Mix the ginger root, honey, stock, ginger, salt, and pepper in a small bowl. Pour into the slow cooker.
3. Cover the slow cooker and cook on low for 6 to 8 hours, or until the pork is very soft. Serve warm.

Nutritional Info per Serving

calories: 241, fat: 6g, protein: 32g, carbs: 15g, fibre: 6g, sugar: 11g, sodium: 267mg

BBQ Pulled Pork

SERVES 8

| PREP TIME: 12 minutes
| COOK TIME: 4 hours

1.4- to 1.8-kg pork shoulder
240ml water
2 tsps. smoked paprika
1½ tsps. garlic powder
1 tsp. thyme
1 tsp. cayenne pepper (optional)
1 tsp. sea salt
1½ tsps. freshly ground black pepper

1. Combine the paprika, garlic powder, black pepper, cayenne pepper (if using), thyme, and salt in a small bowl, and mix well.
2. Carefully trim any large areas of excess fat from the pork shoulder. Rub the pork with the spice mix on all sides.
3. Arrange the pork in a slow cooker and pour the water around the pork. Cook on high for 4 to 5 hours or on low for 7 to 8 hours.
4. While the meat still warm, shred the pork with two forks.

Nutritional Info per Serving
calories: 396, fat: 23g, protein: 43g, carbs: 1g, fibre: 0g, sugar: 0g, sodium: 419mg

Apples-Onions Pork Chops

SERVES 4

| PREP TIME: 4 minutes
| COOK TIME: 30 minutes

1 tbsp. olive oil
4 pork chops, boneless
1 tsp. salt
1 tsp. cinnamon
¼ tsp. black pepper
3 apples, cored and sliced

1 sweet onion, sliced
120ml low-sodium broth
120ml apple cider
1 tbsp. Dijon mustard
Salt and pepper

1. Preheat the oven to 205ºC.
2. In a large frying pan, heat the oil over medium-high heat.
3. Season the pork chops with the salt, cinnamon, and pepper, then add them to the frying pan. Cook for 4 to 5 minutes per side. Transfer the pork chops to a platter.
4. Add the apples, the onion and extra oil, if needed to the frying pan. Sauté until softened, 3 to 4 minutes.
5. Pour in the broth and apple cider. Stir in the mustard and simmer for 5 minutes until the liquid is reduced by half.
6. Return the pork chops and any juices that have collected on the plate to the frying pan. Place the frying pan in the oven. Cook for 15 minutes until the pork is cooked through. Season with salt and pepper as desired.

Nutritional Info per Serving
calories: 263, fat: 8g, protein: 21g, carbs: 20g, fibre: 2g, sugar: 17g, sodium: 751mg

Classic Moroccan Beef in Lettuce Cups

SERVES 10

| PREP TIME: 21 minutes
| COOK TIME: 9 hours

1.4 kg grass-fed beef sirloin roast
397 g BPA-free can no-salt-added diced tomatoes, undrained
20 butter lettuce leaves
4 radishes, thinly sliced
1 cup grated carrot

65g pomegranate seeds
120ml low-sodium beef stock
55g tomato paste
4 garlic cloves, cut into slivers
1 tsp. ground cinnamon
1 tsp. ground cumin

1. Use a fork to poke holes in the sirloin roast and insert the slivers of garlic. Place the roast into a 5.5 litre slow cooker.
2. Mix the beef stock, tomatoes, tomato paste, cumin, and cinnamon until well blended in a medium bowl. Pour the mixture over the roast.
3. Cover the slow cooker and cook on low for 7 to 9 hours or until the beef is soft.
4. Remove the beef from the slow cooker and use two forks to shred. In a large serving bowl, mix the beef with about 240ml of the liquid from the slow cooker.
5. Serve the beef mixture with the remaining ingredients.

Nutritional Info per Serving

calories: 376, fat: 21g, protein: 35g, carbs: 9g, fibre: 2g, sugar: 5g, sodium: 141mg

Classic Lamb and Aubergine Tikka Masala

SERVES 4

| PREP TIME: 7 minutes
| COOK TIME: 23 minutes

1 tbsp. extra-virgin olive oil
454 g boneless lamb, cut into 2.5cm cubes
425 g can diced tomato
397 g can unsweetened light coconut milk
1 aubergine, diced
½ white onion, finely diced
2 cloves garlic, minced

2 tbsps. tomato paste
1½ tsps. garam masala
1½ tsps. ground cumin
1 tsp. turmeric
¼ tsp. ground coriander
¼ tsp. sea salt, divided

1. In a medium, deep frying pan over medium heat, heat the olive oil. Place the onion and garlic and cook for 2 minutes, or until fragrant. Put the aubergine and ⅛ tsp. of sea salt and sauté for about 5 minutes. Pour in the tomato paste and sauté for 1 minute more. If the aubergine starts to stick, add 2 tbsps. of water. Keep aside.
2. Add the lamb, garam masala, cumin, turmeric, coriander, and remaining ⅛ tsp. of salt in the same frying pan. Cook for about 8 minutes. Place the tomatoes and scrape the bottom of the pan to deglaze. Pour in the coconut milk and take the aubergine back to the frying pan. Mix to combine well, cover, and cook for about 7 minutes.
3. Serve in 4 bowls.

Nutritional Info per Serving

calories: 289, fat: 13g, protein: 26g, carbs: 17g, fibre: 5g, sugar: 10g, sodium: 500mg

Feta Lamb Burgers

SERVES 4

| PREP TIME: 15 minutes
| COOK TIME: 10 minutes

20g sun-dried tomatoes
Cooking oil spray
454 g ground lamb
20g low-sodium feta cheese, crumbled

1 tbsp. tomato paste
½ tsp. cumin
½ tsp. salt
¼ tsp. pepper

1. In a medium bowl, cover sun-dried tomatoes with boiling water and soak until softened, for 10 to 15 minutes. Drain and dice.
2. Preheat the grill to medium. Lightly coat the grill with spray.
3. Combine all of the ingredients and form 4 evenly shaped patties.
4. Grill about 5 minutes per side, until the internal temperature reads 65ºC.

Nutritional Info per Serving

calories: 368, fat: 28g, protein: 20g, carbs: 5g, fibre: 1.3g, sugar: 2.1g, sodium: 617mg

Beef and Mushroom Lo Mein

SERVES 10

| PREP TIME: 20 minutes
| COOK TIME: 10½ hours

907 g grass-fed beef chuck roast, cut into 5cm pieces
227 g package whole-wheat spaghetti pasta, broken in half
250g shiitake mushrooms, sliced
700ml low-sodium beef stock
2 onions, chopped
1 jalapeño pepper, minced
4 garlic cloves, minced
2 tbsps. honey
2 tbsps. low-sodium soy sauce
1 tbsp. grated fresh ginger root

1. Mix the onions, mushrooms, garlic, ginger root, and jalapeño pepper in a 5.5 litre slow cooker. Place the beef cubes and gently stir.
2. In a medium bowl, mix the soy sauce, beef stock, and honey until well combined. Pour the mixture into the slow cooker.
3. Cover the slow cooker and cook on low for 8 to 10 hours, or until the beef is very tender.
4. Turn the slow cooker to high heat. Place the pasta and stir slowly, making sure all of the spaghetti is covered with liquid.
5. Cook on high for about 20 to 30 minutes, or until the pasta is soft. Serve hot.

Nutritional Info per Serving

calories: 355, fat: 14g, protein: 28g, carbs: 33g, fibre: 4g, sugar: 8g, sodium: 294mg

Beef Tenderloin with Onion Marmalade

SERVES 4

| PREP TIME: 23 minutes
| COOK TIME: 1 hour

1 tsp. olive oil, plus more for the grill
2 large red onions, peeled and diced
2 tbsps. unsweetened apple juice
3 tsps. red wine vinegar
2 tbsps. honey
1 tbsp. fresh thyme, chopped
Pinch of salt
Pinch of black pepper, freshly ground
113 g beef tenderloin steaks, each about 2.5cm thick and trimmed of fat

1. In a large saucepan, heat the oil over medium-low heat and sauté the red onion about 40 minutes until very soft and lightly caramelised, stirring frequently.
2. Add the juice, vinegar, honey, thyme, salt, and pepper.
3. Lower the heat and continue to cook, stirring frequently, until most of the liquid evaporates and the marmalade is thick, about 10 minutes.
4. Preheat a barbecue to medium-high heat and brush the grill with olive oil. Alternatively, preheat the broiler and lightly grease a broiling pan.
5. On the barbecue, grill the tenderloin, turning once, until it is the desired doneness, about 5 minutes per side for medium 70°C. Or in the oven, broil the tenderloin until it reaches the desired doneness, turning once, about 6 minutes per side.
6. Transfer the tenderloin to a cutting board and rest for at least 10 minutes. Serve topped with the onion marmalade.

Nutritional Info per Serving

calories: 291, fat: 8g, protein: 35g, carbs: 17g, fibre: 2g, sugar: 13g, sodium: 223mg

CHAPTER 4
VEGETABLES

Red Lentil and Coconut Curry / 27

Roasted Sweet Potato, Carrot and Quinoa

Salad / 27

Vegetable Chilli / 28

Healthy Mushroom Cashew Rice / 28

Turmeric Sweet Potato Soup / 29

Vegetables Chickpea Curry / 29

Tandoori Courgette Cauliflower Curry / 30

Spicy Black Bean, Sweet Potato and Brown

Rice Sliders / 30

Bean Tostadas / 30

Shakshuka with Red Peppers / 31

Cauliflower and CashewGratin / 31

Red Lentil and Coconut Curry

SERVES 6

| PREP TIME: 15 minutes
| COOK TIME: 45 minutes

1 tbsp. coconut oil
1 small sweet onion, peeled and diced
2 tsps. garlic, minced
2 medium carrots, peeled and diced
1 sweet potato, peeled and diced
2 tsps. fresh ginger, grated
1 tbsp. curry powder
3 large ripe tomatoes, diced
470ml fat-free, low-sodium vegetable stock
240ml coconut water
200g dried red lentils, rinsed and picked through
225g finely julienned spinach

1. In a large pot over medium heat, heat the coconut oil and sauté the onion and garlic until softened, about 3 minutes.
2. Add the carrots and sweet potato and sauté for 10 more minutes, stirring often.
3. Add the remaining ingredients except the spinach and stir to combine.
4. Bring the mixture to a boil and then lower the heat.
5. Simmer the curry until most of the water is absorbed and the lentils and vegetables are tender, about 30 minutes.
6. Stir in the spinach and let the curry sit for about 10 minutes.

Nutritional Info per Serving

calories: 288, fat: 5g, protein: 16g, carbs: 34g, fibre: 7g, sugar: 9g, sodium: 60mg

Roasted Sweet Potato, Carrot and Quinoa Salad

SERVES 4

| PREP TIME: 9 minutes
| COOK TIME: 20 minutes

1 tbsp. avocado oil
2 sweet potatoes, cut into 1.25cm dice
2 carrots, peeled and cut into 1.25cm dice
180g quinoa
50g golden raisins
40g slivered almonds
470ml water
Zest and juice of 1 lemon
1 tbsp. cumin
1 tsp. garlic powder
1 tsp. cinnamon
¼ tsp. sea salt
¼ tsp. cardamom

1. Preheat the oven to 220ºC and line a sheet pan with unbleached parchment paper.
2. Combine the sweet potatoes, carrots, avocado oil, garlic powder, cumin, cinnamon, salt, and cardamom in a large bowl. Toss well to coat the vegetables evenly with the seasoning. Take them to the sheet pan, and evenly divide. Roast for 20 minutes, or until tender.
3. When the vegetables are cooking, add 470ml water and the quinoa to a saucepan. Bring to a boil, lower the heat, and simmer for 15 minutes, or until the water is absorbed.
4. Place the cooked quinoa, raisins, and slivered almonds to a bowl and gently toss them in the juice and zest of the lemon. Put the roasted vegetables and toss to combine well. Divide among 4 bowls evenly and serve immediately.

Nutritional Info per Serving

calories: 334, fat: 10g, protein: 10g, carbs: 55g, fibre: 8g, sugar: 10g, sodium: 211mg

Vegetable Chilli

SERVES 12

| PREP TIME: 14 minutes
| COOK TIME: 1 hours

2 tbsps. olive oil
1 large sweet onion, peeled and finely chopped
3 tsps. garlic, minced
2 cups button mushrooms, chopped
2 large carrots, peeled and diced
1 large red bell pepper, seeded and diced
1 large courgette, diced
1 jalapeño pepper, seeded and chopped
30g chilli powder
1 tbsp. cumin, ground

1 tbsp. dried oregano
1 tsp. red pepper flakes,
4 large tomatoes, chopped
170 g can sodium-free tomato paste
240ml fat-free, low-sodium vegetable stock
360g black beans, rinsed and drained
360g red kidney beans, rinsed and drained
360g navy beans, rinsed and drained

1. In a large pot, heat the olive oil over medium-high heat and sauté the onion, garlic, and mushrooms until softened, about 3 minutes.
2. Add the carrots, red bell pepper, and courgette and sauté for 8 minutes.
3. Add the remaining ingredients and stir.
4. Bring the chilli to a boil and then lower the heat.
5. Simmer the vegetables until they are fork-tender and the flavours have mellowed, about 45 minutes.
6. Remove the chilli from the heat. Rest for about 10 minutes before serving.

Nutritional Info per Serving

calories: 408, fat: 6g, protein: 24g, carbs: 69g, fibre: 14g, sugar: 7g, sodium: 54mg

Healthy Mushroom Cashew Rice

SERVES 6

| PREP TIME: 9 minutes
| COOK TIME: 50 minutes

1 tbsp. olive oil
3 celery stalks, chopped
½ small sweet onion, peeled and chopped
2 tsps. garlic, minced
1 cup sliced button mushrooms
400g uncooked brown basmati rice
850ml fat-free, low-sodium vegetable stock
Black pepper, freshly ground
65g cup cashews, chopped

1. In a large saucepan, heat the oil over medium-high heat and sauté the celery, onion, garlic, and mushrooms until they are softened.
2. Add the rice and sauté for 1 minute.
3. Add the stock and bring to a boil, then lower the heat and cover the pot.
4. Simmer the rice until the liquid is absorbed and the rice is tender, about 35 to 40 minutes.
5. Season with pepper to taste. Top with cashews and serve.

Nutritional Info per Serving

calories: 341, fat: 9g, protein: 10g, carbs: 51g, fibre: 9g, sugar: 2g, sodium: 458mg

Turmeric Sweet Potato Soup

SERVES 6

| PREP TIME: 13 minutes
| COOK TIME: 25 minutes

1 tbsp. olive oil
454 g sweet potatoes, cut into 1.25cm dice
3 carrots, cut into 1.25cm dice
950ml low-sodium vegetable broth
470ml water
60ml light coconut milk
1 bunch coriander, chopped

1 white onion, cut into 6.5mm dice
2 tsps. turmeric
1 tsp. cumin
½ tsp. coriander
¼ tsp. freshly ground black pepper

1. In a Dutch oven over medium heat, heat the olive oil. Add the onion and cook for 3 minutes, or until the onion is tender. Place the turmeric, cumin, black pepper, and coriander. Stir for about 1 minute until fragrant.
2. Add the carrots and sweet potatoes and cook for 10 minutes, or until the vegetables are tender. Pour in the vegetable broth and water. Combine well, cover, and sauté for about 5 minutes.
3. Blend the soup to your desired consistency with an immersion blender. Pour in more vegetable broth or water if a thinner consistency is desired. Cook for another 5 minutes. Serve in bowls and swirl in the coconut milk. Garnish with the coriander.

Nutritional Info per Serving

calories: 189, fat: 5g, protein: 3g, carbs: 35g, fibre: 6g, sugar: 5g, sodium: 671mg

Vegetables Chickpea Curry

SERVES 4

| PREP TIME: 15 minutes
| COOK TIME: 23 minutes

1 tbsp. olive oil
425 g can tomatoes
383 g can light coconut milk
2 large potatoes, cut into 1.25cm dice
3 carrots, cut into 6.5mm dice
1 cup chickpeas
1 cup fresh or frozen green peas
1 onion, cut into 6.5mm dice

1 (2.5cm) piece ginger, peeled and grated
2 garlic cloves, minced
1 tbsp. curry powder
1 tsp. garam masala
¼ tsp. sea salt

1. In a Dutch oven over medium heat, heat the olive oil. Place the onion, ginger, and garlic, and cook for 3 minutes, until the onion is tender. Put the curry powder and stir until fragrant.
2. Place the potatoes and carrots and cook for about 6 minutes. Add the chickpeas, peas, tomatoes, and garam masala. Stir in and simmer for about 3 minutes.
3. Toss the coconut milk and salt into the vegetables and simmer for 10 minutes, or until the sauce begins to thicken.
4. Divide among 4 bowls evenly and serve immediately.

Nutritional Info per Serving

calories: 347, fat: 9g, protein: 11g, carbs: 62g, fibre: 14g, sugar: 20g, sodium: 414mg

Tandoori Courgette Cauliflower Curry

SERVES 2

| PREP TIME: 6 minutes
| COOK TIME: 25 minutes

1 tbsp. extra-virgin olive oil
½ head cauliflower, broken into small florets
1 courgette, cubed
1 white onion, sliced

2 garlic cloves, minced
2 to 3 tbsps. tandoori curry paste
¼ tsp. Himalayan salt
¼ cup fresh coriander (optional)

1. In a pot of water, cook the cauliflower florets for about 5 minutes, until tender. Reserve about 470ml of the cooking liquid.
2. In a large saucepan, heat the olive oil over medium heat. Place the onion and garlic. Cook for 2 minutes.
3. Add the courgette and cook for an additional 3 minutes.
4. Place the cauliflower, reserved liquid, curry paste, and salt. Stir, cover, and cook for 15 minutes more.
5. Garnish with fresh coriander, if desired. Serve hot.

Nutritional Info per Serving

calories: 66, fat: 4g, protein: 2g, carbs: 7g, fibre: 3g, sugar: 1g, sodium: 94mg

Spicy Black Bean, Sweet Potato and Brown Rice Sliders

SERVES 6

| PREP TIME: 12 minutes
| COOK TIME: 25 minutes

425 g can black beans, rinsed and drained
12 whole wheat buns
2 medium sweet potatoes
2 avocados, cut into 6.5mm dice
200g frozen brown rice
½ small red onion, cut into 6.5mm dice

2 tbsps. hemp seeds
2 tbsps. chipotle hot sauce
2 tsps. cumin
1 tsp. smoked paprika
¼ tsp. chilli powder
¼ tsp. sea salt

1. Preheat the oven to 205ºC and line a sheet pan with unbleached parchment paper.
2. Use a fork to pierce the sweet potatoes 3 to 4 times and microwave them for about 5 minutes, turning them halfway through.
3. When the potatoes are cooking, place the black beans to a medium bowl. Mash the beans to a slight chunky consistency with a potato masher or fork. Put the rice, onion, paprika, cumin, salt, and chilli powder. Stir well.
4. Once the sweet potatoes are tender, let them cool slightly before carefully spooning out the flesh and putting it to the black bean mixture. Stir well.
5. Shape the potato-bean mixture into 12 (3.5cm) balls. Flatten them to approximately 3.5cm thick, then arrange them evenly on the sheet pan. Bake them for about 10 minutes, flip them, and then bake for an additional 10 minutes. Top with avocado, hemp seeds, and chipotle hot sauce. Serve immediately.

Nutritional Info per Serving

calories: 458, fat: 12g, protein: 19g, carbs: 71g, fibre: 16g, sugar: 4g, sodium: 563mg

Bean Tostadas

SERVES 4

| PREP TIME: 12 minutes
| COOK TIME: 15 minutes

8 (15cm) whole-wheat tortillas
Nonstick cooking spray
540g canned sodium-free black beans, drained and rinsed
1 small sweet onion, peeled and coarsely chopped
1 red bell pepper, seeded and diced

2 jalapeño peppers, seeded and coarsely chopped
1 tsp. cumin, ground
4 tbsps. water
4 tsps. fresh coriander, chopped
55g crumbled low-sodium feta
1 large tomato, diced
75g romaine lettuce, shredded

1. Preheat the oven to 205ºC.
2. On two baking sheets, toast the tortillas in the oven until crisp, about 5 minutes.
3. Remove the tortillas from the baking sheets.
4. Lightly coat the baking sheets with cooking spray. Spread the beans, onion, red pepper, and jalapeño peppers evenly on the sheets. Roast the mixture for about 10 minutes.
5. In a food processor, combine the roasted beans and vegetables with the cumin and water. Process until coarsely chopped.
6. On each tortilla, spread an equal amount of the bean mixture. Sprinkle with the coriander and feta.
7. Top each with the tomato and shredded lettuce.
8. Serve two tostadas per person.

Nutritional Info per Serving

calories: 250, fat: 3g, protein: 11g, carbs: 55g, fibre: 23g, sugar: 2g, sodium: 554mg

Shakshuka with Red Peppers

SERVES 4

| PREP TIME: 8 minutes
| COOK TIME: 23 minutes

1 tbsp. extra-virgin olive oil
1 small white onion, diced
1 medium red bell pepper, cut into thin strips
2 garlic cloves, minced
2 cups kale, chopped
1 tbsp. red wine vinegar
1 tsp. Italian seasoning
½ tsp. black pepper, freshly ground
¼ tsp. red pepper flakes (optional)
¼ tsp. salt
794 g can no-salt-added diced tomatoes with juice
8 large eggs

1. Heat the oil in a large cast-iron or nonstick frying pan over medium heat. Add the onion and cook for 2 to 3 minutes, stirring frequently, until translucent.
2. Add the red bell pepper and cook for 5 minutes, stirring frequently, until the vegetables are soft.
3. Stir in the garlic.
4. Add the kale one handful a time. Cook, stirring continuously, adding more kale as it wilts.
5. Pour in the vinegar, stirring constantly for 1 minute to remove any stuck bits from the bottom.
6. Add the Italian seasoning, black pepper, red pepper flakes (if using), and salt. Stir.
7. Add the diced tomatoes and their juices and stir to fully combined. Cover the frying pan and cook for 5 minutes.
8. Create 8 wells in the sauce with the back of a large spoon. Gently crack 1 egg into each well. Cover the frying pan and cook for 6 minutes, or until the egg whites are set. You may want to slightly undercook the eggs, as they'll continue cooking when reheated.
9. With a serving spoon, portion 2 eggs and one-fourth of the sauce into each of 4 large single-compartment glass meal-prep containers. Cover and refrigerate.

Nutritional Info per Serving
calories: 243, fat: 14g, protein: 15g, carbs: 14g, fibre: 1.8g, sugar: 7g, sodium: 257mg

Cauliflower and CashewGratin

SERVES 4

| PREP TIME: 6 minutes
| COOK TIME: 30 minutes

Nonstick cooking spray
200g bite-size cauliflower florets
240g raw cashews, divided
180ml unsweetened almond milk
15g nutritional yeast, plus 1 tbsp.
240ml low-sodium vegetable broth
3 tbsps. hemp seeds

3 tbsps. almond flour
1¼ tsps. garlic powder, divided
1¼ tsps. onion powder, divided
1 tsp. cumin
¼ tsp. dried parsley
¼ tsp. sea salt, divided

1. Preheat the oven to 205°C and line a 23cm square baking dish with nonstick cooking spray.
2. In a medium saucepan, cover the cauliflower florets with water and bring to a boil over high heat. Lower the heat and simmer for about 5 minutes. Drain the water and keep the cauliflower aside in a large bowl.
3. To make the topping: When the cauliflower is cooking, place 130g cashews, ⅛ tsp. of salt, hemp seeds, parsley, 1 tbsp. of nutritional yeast, ¼ tsp. of onion powder and ¼ tsp. of garlic powder to a food processor or high-speed blender and blend until finely chopped. Keep aside.
4. To make the cashew cheese: Add the remaining ¾ cup cashews, ¼ cup nutritional yeast, 1 tsp. garlic powder, 1 tsp. onion powder, almond milk, vegetable broth, almond flour, and cumin in the food processor or high-speed blender. Blend until smooth.
5. Place the cashew cheese over the cauliflower and mix well. Pour the cauliflower into the sprayed baking dish and cover with the topping. Put in the oven and bake for about 20 minutes. Divide among 4 bowls evenly and serve immediately.

Nutritional Info per Serving
calories: 429, fat: 32g, protein: 17g, carbs: 26g, fibre: 5g, sugar: 8g, sodium: 357mg

CHAPTER 5
POULTRY

Sheet-Pan Chicken Fajitas / 33

Chicken Marinara Meatballs / 33

Chicken Enchiladas / 34

Jerk Chicken Thigh / 34

Oven Chicken Thighs with Paprika / 35

Peachy Chicken Picante / 35

Balsamic Chicken Caprese Bowl / 36

Classic Jambalaya / 36

Savoury Chicken Bruschetta Pasta / 36

Chicken with Squash and Mushroom / 37

Delicious Chicken Marsala / 37

Sheet-Pan Chicken Fajitas

SERVES 4-6

| PREP TIME: 6 minutes
| COOK TIME: 30 minutes

680 to 907 g chicken breast, sliced
3 bell peppers (assorted colours), sliced
1 red onion, sliced
1 tbsp. avocado oil
1 tbsp. taco seasoning

1. Preheat the oven to 205°C. Line a baking sheet with parchment paper.
2. Mix together all of the ingredients in a large bowl until evenly coated.
3. Pour the chicken mixture on the baking sheet in a layer. Bake for 30 minutes or until the chicken is cooked through.

Nutritional Info per Serving

calories: 241, fat: 6g, protein: 34g, carbs: 9g, fibre: 1.7g, sugar: 4g, sodium: 442mg

Chicken Marinara Meatballs

SERVES 6

| PREP TIME: 7 minutes
| COOK TIME: 20 minutes

454 g ground chicken
1 large egg, beaten
950ml marinara sauce (no sugar added)
120g almond or oat flour
30g grated low-fat Parmesan cheese, plus more for garnish
1 tbsp. chopped fresh basil, plus more for garnish
½ tsp. garlic powder

1. Preheat the oven to 220°C. Gently line a large rimmed baking sheet with parchment paper.
2. Combine the ground chicken, flour, egg, Parmesan, basil, and garlic powder in a large bowl. Mix well to incorporate the ingredients entirely.
3. Shape the mixture into small, 2.5cm meatballs and arrange on the baking sheet. Bake for about 10 minutes, until the chicken is cooked through.
4. Meanwhile, in a large, deep sauté pan or frying pan, warm the marinara sauce over medium heat.
5. Place the cooked meatballs to the sauce. Allow the meatballs to simmer in the sauce for 5 to 10 minutes. Top with additional Parmesan cheese and chopped basil, if desired. Serve warm.

Nutritional Info per Serving

calories: 260, fat: 16g, protein: 24g, carbs: 9g, fibre: 2g, sugar: 6g, sodium: 543mg

Chicken Enchiladas

SERVES 6

| PREP TIME: 13 minutes
| COOK TIME: 25 minutes

Cooking oil spray
454 g mild salsa verde, divided
250g cooked, shredded chicken
1 green bell pepper, diced
1 small red onion, diced

12 corn tortillas
90g low-fat Cheddar cheese, shredded
1 tomato, diced
1 avocado, diced
1 jalapeño, diced

1. Preheat the oven to 205°C. Coat the inside of a 23 by 33 cm baking dish with cooking spray.
2. Reserve 60ml plus 2 tbsps. of salsa verde.
3. Mix together the chicken, bell pepper, onion, and the remaining salsa verde in a large bowl.
4. Spread the 60ml of reserved salsa verde evenly on the baking dish.
5. Wrap the tortillas in a damp paper towel. Microwave for 30 seconds to soften.
6. Pour about ⅛ of the chicken mixture in the center of the tortilla. Roll up the tortilla and bake in the baking dish, seam-side down. Repeat with all of the tortillas.
7. Top the rolled tortillas with the remaining 2 tbsps. of salsa verde. Sprinkle with cheese, and cover the baking dish with foil. Bake for 20 minutes, then remove the foil and broil for 1 to 2 minutes.
8. Top with tomato, avocado, and jalapeño before serving!

Nutritional Info per Serving

calories: 568, fat: 22g, protein: 35g, carbs: 47g, fibre: 8g, sugar: 4.6g, sodium: 645mg

Jerk Chicken Thigh

SERVES 6

| PREP TIME: 13 minutes
| COOK TIME: 9 hours

113 g boneless, skinless chicken thighs
3 onions, chopped
6 garlic cloves, minced
120ml freshly squeezed orange juice
3 tbsps. grated fresh ginger root
2 tbsps. honey
1 tbsp. chilli powder
1 tsp. ground red chilli
½ tsp. ground cloves
¼ tsp. ground allspice

1. Cut slashes across the chicken thighs so the flavourings can permeate.
2. Mix the honey, ginger root, ground chilli, chilli powder, cloves, and allspice in a small bowl. Gently rub this mixture into the chicken. Allow the chicken to stand while you make the vegetables.
3. Place the onions and garlic in a 5.5 litre slow cooker. Then top with the chicken. Add the orange juice over all. Cover the slow cooker and cook on low for 7 to 9 hours, or until a food thermometer registers 75°C. Serve warm.

Nutritional Info per Serving

calories: 184, fat: 3g, protein: 30g, carbs: 11g, fibre: 1g, sugar: 7g, sodium: 316mg

Oven Chicken Thighs with Paprika

SERVES 6

| PREP TIME: 7 minutes
| COOK TIME: 45 minutes

Cooking oil spray
907 g boneless, skinless chicken thighs
60g almond butter
5 to 6 garlic cloves, minced
2 tbsps. paprika
1 tbsp. oregano
½ tsp. red pepper flakes
½ tsp. dried parsley
¼ tsp. salt
¼ tsp. pepper

1. Preheat the oven to 220°C. Coat the inside of a 23 by 33 cm baking dish with spray.
2. Pat the chicken thighs dry and place them in the baking dish.
3. In a small saucepan, heat the almond butter and whisk in the garlic, paprika, oregano, red pepper flakes, parsley, salt, and pepper. Brush the sauce over the chicken thighs.
4. Bake for 40 to 45 minutes to internal temperature of 75°C.

Nutritional Info per Serving

calories: 274, fat: 18g, protein: 21g, carbs: 4g, fibre: 0.7g, sugar: 0.2g, sodium: 334mg

Peachy Chicken Picante

SERVES 4

| PREP TIME: 11 minutes
| COOK TIME: 43 minutes

1 tbsp. almond butter
1 red onion, diced
3 garlic cloves, minced
1 jalapeño, seeded and diced
4 peaches, chopped
411 g can diced tomatoes (no sugar added)
1 tbsp. honey
½ tsp. salt
½ tsp. pepper
¼ tsp. red pepper flakes (optional)
454 g chicken breast

1. Preheat the oven to 205°C.
2. In a large, oven-safe frying pan, heat the ghee over medium heat. Add the onion and sauté for 3 to 5 minutes, or until softened. Add the garlic, jalapeño, and peaches. Sauté for 2 to 3 minutes more.
3. Add the tomatoes, honey, salt, pepper, and red pepper flakes (if using) and simmer for 5 minutes. Add the chicken. Spoon or brush the sauce over the chicken to ensure it completely coated with sauce. Place the frying pan in the oven and cook for 30 minutes, or until internal temperature of the chicken reaches 75°C.

Nutritional Info per Serving

calories: 234, fat: 5g, protein: 24g, carbs: 22g, fibre: 3g, sugar: 18g, sodium: 703mg

Balsamic Chicken Caprese Bowl

SERVES 4

| PREP TIME: 15 minutes
| COOK TIME: 14 minutes

For the Balsamic Vinaigrette:
2 tbsps. olive oil
3 tbsps. balsamic vinegar
½ tsp. sea salt
¼ tsp. ground black pepper
For the Chicken:
1 tbsp. olive oil
680 g boneless, skinless chicken breasts

⅛ tsp. garlic powder
½ tsp. sea salt
¼ tsp. ground black pepper
For the Bowl:
4 medium courgettes, spiralized
400g cherry tomatoes, halved
225g diced fresh nonfat mozzarella
8 basil leaves, for garnish

Make the Vinaigrette:
1. Combine the balsamic vinegar, olive oil, salt, and pepper in a small mixing bowl. Bring the ingredients together with a whisk or a fork, until the dressing is emulsified.

Make the Chicken:
2. In a large frying pan, heat the olive oil over medium-high heat. Sprinkle the chicken with the salt, pepper, and garlic powder. Cook the chicken in the pan for about 4 to 6 minutes on each side, until golden brown and cooked through. Then take the chicken from the heat, leaving behind any remaining oil. Let the chicken to sit for 5 minutes, then slice it, and keep it aside.

Make the Bowl:
3. Place the courgettes to the same pan you used to cook the chicken. Sauté the courgettes over medium-high heat for about 2 to 3 minutes, until it's tender, but not mushy.
4. Combine the mozzarella and tomatoes in a medium bowl. Slice the basil leaves.
5. To assemble the bowls, begin with a layer of the courgettes, topped with the sliced chicken and then the cheese-tomato mixture. Pour the balsamic vinaigrette over the top and sprinkle with the basil. Enjoy!

Nutritional Info per Serving

calories: 363, fat: 15g, protein: 48g, carbs: 7g, fibre: 2g, sugar: 5g, sodium: 565mg

Classic Jambalaya

SERVES 6-8

| PREP TIME: 20 minutes
| COOK TIME: 9½ hours

680 g raw shrimp, shelled and deveined
113 g boneless, skinless chicken thighs, cut into 5cm pieces
5 celery stalks, sliced
2 jalapeño peppers, minced
2 green bell peppers, stemmed, seeded, and chopped

470ml low-sodium chicken stock
2 onions, chopped
6 garlic cloves, minced
1 tbsp. Cajun seasoning
¼ tsp. cayenne pepper

1. Mix the chicken, onions, garlic, jalapeños, bell peppers, celery, chicken stock, Cajun seasoning, and cayenne in a 5.5 litre slow cooker. Cover the slow cooker and cook on low for 7 to 9 hours, or until the chicken registers 75ºC on a food thermometer.
2. Stir in the shrimp. Cover and cook for an additional 30 to 40 minutes, or until the shrimp are curled and pink. Serve warm.

Nutritional Info per Serving

calories: 417, fat: 20g, protein: 34g, carbs: 27g, fibre: 3g, sugar: 3g, sodium: 385mg

Savoury Chicken Bruschetta Pasta

SERVES 4

| PREP TIME: 13 minutes
| COOK TIME: 16 minutes

For the Pasta and Tomatoes:
227 g whole wheat angel hair pasta
2 cups tomatoes, diced
7g fresh basil, thinly sliced
15g red onion, finely chopped
3 garlic cloves, minced
1 tbsp. balsamic vinegar
1 tbsp. olive oil
¼ tsp. salt

¼ tsp. pepper
For the Chicken:
680 g chicken breast, sliced
2 tbsps. olive oil, divided
½ tsp. dried basil
½ tsp. salt
¼ tsp. pepper
Fresh basil leaves, low-fat Parmesan cheese, red pepper flakes, for topping (optional)

Make the Pasta and Tomatoes:
1. Bring salted water to boil over high heat. Add the pasta and cook according to the package instructions. When the pasta is cooked, drain.
2. Meanwhile, in a medium bowl, toss together the tomatoes, basil, onion, garlic, vinegar, oil, salt, and pepper.

Make the Chicken:
3. Combine the chicken with 1 tbsp. of the oil, basil, salt, and pepper in a medium bowl.
4. In a large frying pan, heat the remaining 1 tbsp. olive oil over medium heat. Add the chicken and sauté until cooked through.
5. Add tomato mixture to frying pan with chicken and cook for 3 minutes. Add the pasta to the frying pan and fold the ingredients together gently with tongs.
6. Top with basil, Parmesan, and red pepper flakes, if desired.

Nutritional Info per Serving

calories: 487, fat: 15g, protein: 41g, carbs: 48g, fibre: 2.6g, sugar: 2.8g, sodium: 517mg

Chicken with Squash and Mushroom

SERVES 10

| PREP TIME: 18 minutes
| COOK TIME: 8 hours

1.4 kg butternut squash, peeled, seeded, and cut into 2.5cm pieces
454 g acorn squash, peeled, seeded, and cut into 2.5cm pieces
170 g bone-in, skinless chicken breasts
227 g package cremini mushrooms, sliced
2 fennel bulbs, cored and sliced
240ml low-sodium chicken stock
120ml canned unsweetened coconut milk
3 sprigs fresh thyme
1 bay leaf
2 tbsps. lemon juice

1. Mix the butternut squash, acorn squash, fennel, mushrooms, chicken, thyme, bay leaf, chicken stock, and coconut milk in a 5.5 litre slow cooker. Cover the slow cooker and cook on low for 6 to 8 hours, or until the chicken registers 75°C on a food thermometer.
2. Remove the thyme sprigs and bay leaf and discard. Stir in the lemon juice and serve warm.

Nutritional Info per Serving

calories: 330, fat: 8g, protein: 43g, carbs: 21g, fibre: 4g, sugar: 3g, sodium: 67mg

Delicious Chicken Marsala

SERVES 4-6

| PREP TIME: 9 minutes
| COOK TIME: 25 minutes

454 to 680 g chicken breasts	15g diced white onion
½ tsp. salt	3 garlic cloves, minced
¼ tsp. pepper	120ml Marsala wine
3 tbsps. cornflour, divided	120ml low-sodium chicken or beef broth
2 tbsps. almond butter	2 tbsps. parsley, fresh
227 g white button mushrooms, sliced	Salt and pepper

1. Place the chicken, salt, pepper, and 2 tbsps. of the cornflour in a large freezer bag and seal. Shake or massage the bag to better coat the chicken.
2. In a large frying pan, heat the butter over medium-high heat. Remove the chicken from the bag and shake off any extra cornflour. Place the chicken in the frying pan and cook for 2 to 3 minutes until brown-coloured per side. Transfer the chicken to a plate.
3. Add the mushrooms to the frying pan and sauté for 2 to 3 minutes. Add the onion and garlic and sauté for 1 to 2 minutes.
4. Pour in the wine, broth, and remaining tbsp. of cornflour. Stir, scraping up any brown bits from the sides and bottom of the frying pan. Bring to a boil.
5. Reduce the heat to medium and return the chicken to the frying pan. Cover and simmer for 15 minutes, or until the chicken is cooked through and the sauce has thickened.
6. Garnish with the parsley and season with the salt and pepper to taste before serving.

Nutritional Info per Serving

calories: 254, fat: 8g, protein: 24g, carbs: 12g, fibre: 0.7g, sugar: 1.8g, sodium: 602mg

CHAPTER 6
SALAD

Cherry Tomato and Avocado Salad / 39

Roasted Beet and Pistachio Salad / 39

Roasted Red Pepper and Parsley Salad / 40

Lemon Avocado Tuna Salad / 40

Greek Cherry Tomato Quinoa Salad / 41

Rocket Watermelon and Avocado Salad / 41

Baked Acorn Squash and Rocket Salad / 42

Flavourful Mango and Bean Salad / 42

Caprese Salad Quinoa Bowl / 42

Chickpea Salad with Olives and Cucumber / 43

Tasteful Quinoa Tabboule / 43

Cherry Tomato and Avocado Salad

SERVES 4

| PREP TIME: 9 minutes
| COOK TIME: 0 minutes

340 g multi-coloured cherry or grape tomatoes
1 large ripe avocado, peeled and pitted
15g very thinly sliced red onion
28 g low-sodium queso blanco or feta cheese, crumbled
1 to 2 tbsps. freshly squeezed lime juice (juice of ½ lime)
1 tbsp. chopped fresh coriander
¼ tsp. kosher salt

1. Chop the tomatoes and avocado into equal bite-size pieces and place in a large bowl.
2. Put the onion, cheese, lime juice, coriander, and salt and toss to combine well. Serve right away.

Nutritional Info per Serving

calories: 123, fat: 9g, protein: 3g, carbs: 9g, fibre: 4g, sugar. 3g, sodium: 237mg

Roasted Beet and Pistachio Salad

SERVES 4

| PREP TIME: 5 minutes
| COOK TIME: 30 minutes

3 tbsps. extra-virgin olive oil, divided
4 medium beetroot, quartered
40g pistachios, chopped
60g low-sodium goat cheese, crumbled
2 tbsps. rice vinegar
¼ tsp. Himalayan salt

1. Preheat the oven to 205°C.
2. Mix 2 tbsps. of olive oil with the rice vinegar and salt in a bowl. Keep aside.
3. Line a baking sheet with parchment paper. Gently toss the beetroot with the remaining tbsp. of olive oil and place on the baking sheet.
4. Cover with another sheet of parchment paper and bake for 25 to 30 minutes, until the beetroot are tender.
5. Allow the beetroot to cool and take them to a bowl.
6. Toss the beetroot in the olive oil dressing and transfer to a serving plate.
7. Put goat cheese and pistachios on top. Enjoy!

Nutritional Info per Serving

calories: 188, fat: 15g, protein: 4g, carbs: 10g, fibre: 3g, sugar: 6g, sodium: 175mg

Roasted Red Pepper and Parsley Salad

SERVES 3

| PREP TIME: 2 minutes
| COOK TIME: 30 minutes

2 tbsps. extra-virgin olive oil
6 long red peppers, washed and patted dry
1 tbsp. white wine vinegar
1 tbsp. fresh parsley, chopped, for garnish
¼ tsp. Himalayan salt, plus more as needed

1. Turn on the broiler and let it preheat while you cook the peppers.
2. Line a baking sheet with parchment paper and place the peppers in a single layer, skin-side up.
3. Broil the peppers on one side for about 5 minutes, until the skin starts bubbling. Gently flip the peppers and broil on the other side.
4. Keep turning until all sides of the pepper are brown and the skin is lifted up. This should take about 15 to 20 minutes, depending on your oven.
5. Remove the peppers from the oven and cover the baking sheet with a kitchen towel. Let stand for about 10 minutes.
6. Peel the skin off the peppers and put them flat on a serving plate.
7. Drizzle with the vinegar, oil, and salt. Use clean hands to toss gently so the dressing is evenly applied.
8. Scatter with a little salt and parsley.
9. Serve immediately or refrigerate for 15 minutes to cool further.

Nutritional Info per Serving
calories: 186, fat: 10g, protein: 3g, carbs: 21g, fibre: 7g, sugar: 4g, sodium: 118mg

Lemon Avocado Tuna Salad

SERVES 4

| PREP TIME: 7 minutes
| COOK TIME: 0 minutes

1 tbsp. extra-virgin olive oil
1 avocado, peeled, pitted, and diced
170g wild-caught tuna, drained
15g thinly sliced red onion
Juice and zest of 1 lemon
1 tsp. sea salt
½ tsp. freshly ground black pepper

1. In a medium bowl, add the tuna and break it into chunks with a fork.
2. Place the olive oil, diced avocado, red onion, lemon juice and zest, salt, and pepper. Toss gently.
3. Serve immediately over greens.

Nutritional Info per Serving
calories: 158, fat: 7g, protein: 17g, carbs: 5g, fibre: 3g, sugar: 0g, sodium: 755mg

Greek Cherry Tomato Quinoa Salad

SERVES 4-6

| PREP TIME: 5 minutes
| COOK TIME: 25 minutes

For the Dressing:
60ml extra-virgin olive oil
Juice of ½ large lemon
½ tsp. Himalayan salt

For the Quinoa:
360g quinoa
250g cherry tomatoes, quartered
75g English cucumber, cubed
90g Kalamata olives, chopped
950ml water

1. For the dressing: Whisk together the oil, lemon juice, and salt in a bowl, and keep aside.
2. For the quinoa: Rinse the quinoa under cold water until the water runs clear.
3. Bring 950ml of water to a boil in a medium saucepan.
4. Place the quinoa, cover, and simmer on low for 20 minutes.
5. Open the pot, fluff the quinoa with a fork, cover, and allow it to rest for 5 minutes.
6. Take the quinoa to a large wooden or glass salad bowl and let it cool.
7. Once the quinoa cools to room temperature, put the tomatoes, cucumbers, and olives. Stir to combine well.
8. Add the dressing and toss well. Enjoy!

Nutritional Info per Serving

calories: 311, fat: 14g, protein: 9g, carbs: 39g, fibre: 5g, sugar: 1g, sodium: 184mg

Rocket Watermelon and Avocado Salad

SERVES 1-2

| PREP TIME: 5 minutes
| COOK TIME: 0 minutes

2 tbsps. extra-virgin olive oil
80g rocket
150g watermelon, cubed
¼ avocado, sliced
60g low-sodium goat cheese, crumbled
1 tbsp. balsamic vinegar
⅛ tsp. sea salt (optional)

1. Toss the rocket and olive oil in a bowl.
2. Add the watermelon, avocado, goat cheese, and salt (if using), and toss gently.
3. Pour balsamic vinegar on top and serve right away.

Nutritional Info per Serving

calories: 462, fat: 41g, protein: 10g, carbs: 17g, fibre: 6g, sugar: 9g, sodium: 158mg

Baked Acorn Squash and Rocket Salad

SERVES 2-3

| PREP TIME: 5 minutes
| COOK TIME: 0 minutes

Extra-virgin olive oil, for coating squash
80g rocket
1 medium acorn squash, cut into rounds
80g Brussels sprouts, shaved or thinly sliced
40g cup pomegranate seeds
30g pumpkin seeds

1. Preheat the oven to 205°C.
2. Line a baking sheet with parchment paper. Arrange the acorn squash on the baking sheet and slowly toss with olive oil to coat well. Place in a single layer and bake for about 20 to 25 minutes, until squash is tender.
3. Meanwhile, combine the rocket, Brussels sprouts, pomegranate, and pumpkin seeds in a bowl, and toss with the dressing of choice.
4. Place acorn squash on top and drizzle additional dressing on top. Enjoy!

Nutritional Info per Serving

calories: 351, fat: 22g, protein: 8g, carbs: 34g, fibre: 7g, sugar: 5g, sodium: 352mg

Flavourful Mango and Bean Salad

SERVES 6

| PREP TIME: 9 minutes
| COOK TIME: 0 minutes

2 ripe mangoes, peeled, pitted, and diced
360g low-sodium black beans, rinsed well and drained
2 spring onions, chopped finely
1 small red bell pepper, seeded and diced
1 large ripe tomato, seeded and diced
70g cooked barley
5g fresh coriander, chopped
2 tbsps. fresh lime juice
Black pepper, freshly ground, to taste

1. In a large bowl, combine all the ingredients.
2. Toss to mix and chill in the fridge for about 1 hour before serving.

Nutritional Info per Serving

calories: 239, fat: 5g, protein: 8g, carbs: 38g, fibre: 9g, sugar: 13g, sodium: 207mg

Caprese Salad Quinoa Bowl

SERVES 2

| PREP TIME: 10 minutes
| COOK TIME: 0 minutes

185g cooked quinoa, cooled completely
113 g baby spinach
20g fresh basil, roughly chopped
2 tbsps. extra-virgin olive oil
1 tbsp. lemon juice, freshly squeezed
200g cherry tomatoes, diced
170 g fresh low-fat mozzarella, diced
1 tsp. balsamic glaze

1. In a large bowl, place the spinach and basil.
2. In a small bowl, whisk the oil and lemon juice to combine. Portion the dressing evenly into 2 stainless-steel salad dressing containers.
3. Evenly divide the greens into 2 large glass meal-prep containers with lids. Top with the cooked quinoa, diced tomatoes, and mozzarella. Drizzle each with ½ tsp. of balsamic glaze. Cover and refrigerate.

Nutritional Info per Serving

calories: 532, fat: 32g, protein: 21g, carbs: 28g, fibre: 4g, sugar: 7g, sodium: 67mg

Chickpea Salad with Olives and Cucumber

SERVES 4

| PREP TIME: 13 minutes
| COOK TIME: 0 minutes

For the Dressing:
80ml extra-virgin olive oil
2½ tbsps. freshly squeezed lemon juice
1 tsp. honey
1 tsp. Dijon mustard
Sea salt
Freshly ground black pepper
For the Salad:
439 g can chickpeas, drained and rinsed
80g baby rocket
180g Kalamata olives, sliced
150g diced English cucumber
200g cherry tomatoes, halved
150g low-fat feta cheese

Make the Dressing:
1. In a small bowl, whisk the olive oil, lemon juice, honey, Dijon mustard, salt, and pepper until well combined. Alternatively, pour in a small Mason jar, seal, and shake vigorously until well combined. Keep aside.
Make the Salad:
2. Distribute the chickpeas, rocket, tomatoes, cucumber, olives, and feta equally among 4 bowls.
3. Top each bowl with 1 to 2 tbsps. of dressing and serve.

Nutritional Info per Serving
calories: 386, fat: 27g, protein: 10g, carbs: 26g, fibre: 6g, sugar: 6g, sodium: 472mg

Tasteful Quinoa Tabbouleh

SERVES 8

| PREP TIME: 8 minutes
| COOK TIME: 15 minutes

185g quinoa, uncooked
470ml water
227 g cherry tomatoes, quartered
1 cucumber, chopped
175g chopped roasted red peppers
113 g low-fat feta cheese, crumbled
75g red onion, diced
Juice of 1 lemon
1 tbsp. olive oil
15g parsley fresh, chopped
Salt and pepper

1. Place the quinoa and water in a medium saucepan and bring to a boil. Reduce the heat to low, cover, and cook for 15 minutes, or until all of the water has been absorbed. Mash up with a fork.
2. Combine the cooked quinoa with the remaining ingredients in a large bowl and mix well.
3. Chill in the fridge until ready to serve.

Nutritional Info per Serving
calories: 162, fat: 7g, protein: 5g, carbs: 20g, fibre: 5g, sugar: 4g, sodium: 226mg

CHAPTER 7

FISH AND SEAFOOD

Maple Cedar Plank Salmon / 45

Mushroom Shrimp Scampi / 45

White Fish and Spinach Risotto / 46

Baked Salmon and Asparagus / 46

Tuna and Carrot Salad / 47

Salmon and Veggies Ratatouille / 47

Quick Grilled Ahi Tuna / 48

Parmesan Salmon with Root Vegetables / 48

Tuna and Spinach Burgers / 48

Crispy Mahi-Mahi Tenders / 49

Salmon, Mushroom and Barley Bake / 49

Maple Cedar Plank Salmon

SERVES 4

| PREP TIME: 13 minutes
| COOK TIME: 25 minutes

1 to 2 cedar planks
60ml 100% pure maple syrup
2 tbsps. lemon juice
1 tbsp. Dijon mustard
1 tbsp. soy sauce
½ tsp. garlic powder
1 tsp. paprika
170 g salmon fillets, cleaned and deboned
¼ tsp. salt
¼ tsp. pepper
Lemon juice, freshly squeezed

1. Soak the cedar planks for at least 1 hour prior to grilling. Place the planks in a baking dish and cover with water. They will float, so weigh them down with something like a teapot or a heavy bowl to keep submerged.
2. Heat a large saucepan over medium heat. Whisk together the maple syrup, lemon juice, mustard, soy sauce, garlic powder, and paprika and bring to a boil. When the sauce thickens, after 3 to 5 minutes. Remove the sauce from the heat.
3. Heat the grill to medium-high when the cedar plank has fully soaked.
4. Rub the salmon fillets with salt and pepper and place them skin-side down on the cedar plank.
5. Brush the salmon fillets with the maple glaze.
6. Place the cedar plank with the salmon on the grill. Cook for 15 to 20 minutes or until internal temperature reaches 65°C.

Nutritional Info per Serving

calories: 476, fat: 17g, protein: 58g, carbs: 14g, fibre: 0.2g, sugar: 12g, sodium: 586mg

Mushroom Shrimp Scampi

SERVES 8-10

| PREP TIME: 22 minutes
| COOK TIME: 7½ hours

2 tbsps. clarified butter
907 g raw shrimp, shelled and deveined
454 g cremini mushrooms, sliced
2 leeks, chopped
240ml low-sodium fish stock
60ml freshly squeezed lemon juice
2 onions, chopped
8 garlic cloves, minced
1 tsp. dried basil leaves
Tagliatelle, cooked

1. Mix the mushrooms, onions, leeks, garlic, fish stock, lemon juice, and basil in a 5.5 litre slow cooker. Cover the slow cooker and cook on low for 5 to 7 hours, or until the vegetables are soft.
2. Gently stir in the shrimp. Cover and cook on high for 30 to 40 minutes, or until the shrimp are curled and pink.
3. Stir in the butter. Cover and allow to stand for about 10 minutes, then serve with tagliatelle.

Nutritional Info per Serving

calories: 158, fat: 4g, protein: 22g, carbs: 10g, fibre: 2g, sugar: 3g, sodium: 275mg

White Fish and Spinach Risotto

SERVES 4

| PREP TIME: 7 minutes
| COOK TIME: 5 hours

400g short-grain brown rice
227 g cremini mushrooms, sliced
142 g tilapia fillets
60g baby spinach leaves
60g grated low-sodium Parmesan cheese
1.5l low-sodium vegetable broth or fish stock
2 onions, chopped
5 garlic cloves, minced
2 tbsps. unsalted butter
1 tsp. dried thyme leaves

1. Mix the mushrooms, onions, garlic, rice, thyme, and vegetable broth in a 5.5 litre slow cooker. Cover the slow cooker and cook on low for 3 to 4 hours, or until the rice is soft.
2. Place the fish on top of the rice. Cover and cook for 25 to 35 minutes more, or until the fish flakes when tested with a fork.
3. Gently place the fish into the risotto. Then put the baby spinach leaves.
4. Stir in the butter and cheese. Cover and allow to cook on low for 10 minutes, then serve warm.

Nutritional Info per Serving

calories: 469, fat: 12g, protein: 34g, carbs: 61g, fibre: 5g, sugar: 2g, sodium: 346mg

Baked Salmon and Asparagus

SERVES 4

| PREP TIME: 4 minutes
| COOK TIME: 25 minutes

1 tbsp. extra-virgin olive oil
4 salmon fillets
2 bunches asparagus (about 24 pieces), woody ends cut off
1 tbsp. sesame seeds
1 tbsp. freshly grated nonfat Parmesan cheese
¼ tsp. garlic powder
¾ tsp. Himalayan salt, divided
Freshly ground black pepper (optional)

1. Preheat the oven to 205ºC. Carefully line 2 baking sheets or dishes with parchment paper (one for asparagus and one for salmon).
2. Spread the salmon fillets on a prepared baking sheet and scatter with ½ tsp. of salt and sesame seeds.
3. Bake for about 12 to 15 minutes, then remove from the oven and allow it to rest while you prepare the asparagus.
4. Place asparagus to the other baking sheet, scatter with the remaining ¼ tsp. of salt and garlic powder. Drizzle with the olive oil and toss with hands until evenly coated.
5. Bake for about 10 minutes, until tender.
6. In the last 2 minutes of baking, place the Parmesan cheese on top.
7. Season with black pepper before serving, if desired. Serve the salmon surrounded by asparagus. Enjoy!

Nutritional Info per Serving

calories: 269, fat: 14g, protein: 31g, carbs: 4g, fibre: 2g, sugar: 2g, sodium: 262mg

Tuna and Carrot Salad

SERVES 2

| PREP TIME: 6 minutes
| COOK TIME: 0 minutes

241g tuna packed in olive oil
50g shredded carrots
20g parsley, chopped
30g maize
2 spring onions, chopped (green and white parts)
1 tbsp. Dijon mustard
Avocado slices (optional)
¼ tsp. Himalayan salt

1. Combine the tuna with all the oil from the can, carrots, maize, parsley, spring onions, Dijon mustard, and salt in a medium bowl. Mix well.
2. Serve with avocado slices on top, if desired.

Nutritional Info per Serving
calories: 205, fat: 8g, protein: 27g, carbs: 4g, fibre: 2g, sugar: 0g, sodium: 315mg

Salmon and Veggies Ratatouille

SERVES 8

| PREP TIME: 20 minutes
| COOK TIME: 7½ hours

2 tbsps. olive oil
907 g salmon fillets
5 large tomatoes, seeded and chopped
2 zucchini, peeled and chopped
180g sliced button mushrooms
2 red bell peppers, stemmed, seeded, and chopped
2 onions, chopped
5 garlic cloves, minced
1 tsp. dried herbes de Provence

1. Mix the aubergines, tomatoes, mushrooms, onions, bell peppers, garlic, olive oil, and herbes de Provence in a 5.5 litre slow cooker. Cover the slow cooker and cook on low for 6 to 7 hours, or until the vegetables are soft.
2. Place the salmon to the slow cooker. Cover and cook on low for another 30 to 40 minutes, or until the salmon flakes when tested with a fork.
3. Gently toss the salmon into the vegetables and serve warm.

Nutritional Info per Serving
calories: 342, fat: 16g, protein: 32g, carbs: 18g, fibre: 7g, sugar: 10g, sodium: 218mg

Quick Grilled Ahi Tuna

SERVES 2

| PREP TIME: 15 minutes
| COOK TIME: 5 minutes

For the Marinade:
1 tbsp. sesame oil
2 tbsps. soy sauce
1 tbsp. rice vinegar

For the Tuna:
170 g ahi tuna steaks
Sesame seeds (optional)

1. Preheat the grill to the highest setting.
2. To make the marinade: Whisk together the soy sauce, sesame oil, and rice vinegar in a small bowl.
3. To make the tuna: Wash the tuna steaks and pat them dry with a paper towel. Place the steaks to a bowl, and put the marinade on top. Rub the steaks on both sides to coat well. Leave at room temperature for 15 minutes.
4. Grill the steaks for about 3 minutes on one side and 2 minutes on the other. The steaks will be seared on the outside and pink on the inside.
5. Slice thin with a fork and serve alongside a large green salad of your choice. Garnish with some sesame seeds, if desired.

Nutritional Info per Serving

calories: 256, fat: 8g, protein: 43g, carbs: 1g, fibre: 0g, sugar: 0g, sodium: 455mg

Parmesan Salmon with Root Vegetables

SERVES 6

| PREP TIME: 12 minutes
| COOK TIME: 9 hours

4 large carrots, sliced
4 Yukon Gold potatoes, cubed
2 sweet potatoes, peeled and cubed
142 g salmon fillets
30g grated nonfat Parmesan cheese
2 onions, chopped

3 garlic cloves, minced
80ml low-sodium vegetable broth or fish stock
1 tsp. dried thyme leaves
½ tsp. salt

1. Mix carrots, sweet potatoes, Yukon Gold potatoes, onions, garlic, vegetable broth, thyme, and salt in a 5.5 litre slow cooker. Cover the slow cooker and cook on low for 7 to 9 hours, or until the vegetables are soft.
2. Place the salmon fillets and scatter each with some of the cheese. Cover and cook on low for another 30 to 40 minutes, or until the salmon flakes when tested with a fork. Serve warm.

Nutritional Info per Serving

calories: 491, fat: 19g, protein: 42g, carbs: 38g, fibre: 5g, sugar: 8g, sodium: 560mg

Tuna and Spinach Burgers

SERVES 2-4

| PREP TIME: 4 minutes
| COOK TIME: 7 minutes

2 tbsps. extra-virgin olive oil
241 g can tuna in water, drained
80g cornmeal (polenta)
15gbaby spinach, chopped
1 spring onion, chopped (green and white parts)

1 tbsp. Dijon mustard
½ tsp. Himalayan salt
¼ tsp. freshly ground black pepper

1. Combine the tuna, mustard, spring onion, spinach, cornmeal, salt, and pepper in a small bowl. Mix well.
2. Shape the mixture into 2 large or 4 small patties. Keep aside.
3. In a nonstick sauté pan or frying pan, heat the olive oil over medium heat. Put the burgers and pan-fry on one side for about 3 to 4 minutes, then flip and leave them for 3 minutes more.
4. Take the burgers onto a plate lined with a paper towel to soak up some of the excess olive oil. Enjoy!

Nutritional Info per Serving

calories: 319, fat: 16g, protein: 22g, carbs: 24g, fibre: 3g, sugar: 0g, sodium: 510mg

Crispy Mahi-Mahi Tenders

SERVES 4

| PREP TIME: 6 minutes
| COOK TIME: 18 minutes

Olive oil cooking spray
170 g mahi-mahi fillets, cut into 5cm strips
2 large eggs, beaten
60g tapioca flour
60g almond flour
1 tsp. garlic powder
½ tsp. sea salt
¼ tsp. freshly ground black pepper
Extra-virgin olive oil, for drizzling

1. Preheat the oven to 205°C. Spray a baking sheet lightly with cooking spray.
2. Add the beaten egg into a small bowl. Whisk together the almond flour, tapioca flour, garlic powder, salt and pepper in a medium bowl.
3. Gently dip each mahi strip into the egg mixture and then the dry mixture, turning to coat evenly on all sides.
4. Arrange the strips on the baking sheet and drizzle with olive oil.
5. Bake for about 15 to 18 minutes, until golden, flipping halfway through the baking time. Remove from the oven and serve hot.

Nutritional Info per Serving

calories: 394, fat: 12g, protein: 54g, carbs: 19g, fibre: 2g, sugar: 0g, sodium: 581mg

Salmon, Mushroom and Barley Bake

SERVES 4-6

| PREP TIME: 9 minutes
| COOK TIME: 8½ hours

142 g salmon fillets
300g hulled barley, rinsed
227 g package cremini mushrooms, sliced
2 fennel bulbs, cored and chopped
2 red bell peppers, stemmed, seeded, and chopped
30g grated low-sodium Parmesan cheese
1.2l low-sodium vegetable broth
4 garlic cloves, minced
1 tsp. dried tarragon leaves
⅛ tsp. freshly ground black pepper

1. Mix the barley, fennel, bell peppers, garlic, mushrooms, vegetable broth, tarragon, and pepper in a 5.5 litre slow cooker. Cover the slow cooker and cook on low for 7 to 8 hours, or until the barley has absorbed most of the liquid and is soft, and the vegetables are soft too.
2. Arrange the salmon fillets on top of the barley mixture. Cover and cook on low for 20 to 40 minutes more, or until the salmon flakes when tested with a fork.
3. Stir in the Parmesan cheese, breaking up the salmon, and serve warm.

Nutritional Info per Serving

calories: 609, fat: 20g, protein: 49g, carbs: 55g, fibre: 13g, sugar: 4g, sodium: 441mg

CHAPTER 8
SOUP AND STEWS

Creamy Broccoli and Cauliflower Soup / 51

Salmon Vegetables Chowder / 51

Garlic Roasted Tomato Bisque / 52

Italian Chickpea and Carrot Soup / 52

Pasta Vegetables Stew / 53

Curry Yellow Vegetables / 53

Healthy 15-Bean Soup / 54

French Chicken, Mushroom and Wild Rice

Stew / 54

Quick Lentil Bisque / 54

Healthy Veggie Minestrone Soup / 55

Authentic Ratatouille Soup / 55

Creamy Broccoli and Cauliflower Soup

SERVES 3

| PREP TIME: 4 minutes
| COOK TIME: 23 minutes

1 small head broccoli, broken into florets
½ head cauliflower, broken into florets
1 small carrot, chopped
1 small white onion, cut in half
1 tbsp. low-fat Pecorino Romano cheese

1.5l water
1¾ tsps. Himalayan salt
½ tsp. basil (optional)

1. Combine the broccoli, cauliflower, onion, carrot, salt, basil (if using), and 1.5l water in a medium stockpot.
2. Bring to a boil, then reduce the heat to medium and simmer for about 20 minutes, covered, until the veggies are soft.
3. Drain the water with a colander, reserving 470ml of cooking liquid.
4. Place the vegetables to a high-speed blender with 240ml of the reserved liquid. Gently blend to desired consistency, working in batches, if needed. If you like bisque to be on the thinner side, pour in more of the reserved liquid.
5. Take the bisque back in the pot and bring to a boil.
6. Stir in the cheese, then cover and allow soup to rest for about 3 minutes.
7. Serve hot with some high-fibre crackers or a piece of whole-grain toast.

Nutritional Info per Serving

calories: 106, fat: 2g, protein: 7g, carbs: 19g, fibre: 7g, sugar: 6g, sodium: 430mg

Salmon Vegetables Chowder

SERVES 8-10

| PREP TIME: 15 minutes
| COOK TIME: 8½ hours

907 g skinless salmon fillets
6 medium Yukon Gold potatoes, cut into 5cm pieces
4 large carrots, sliced
180g sliced cremini mushrooms
340g shredded low-sodium Swiss cheese
240ml unsweetened whole milk
2l low-sodium vegetable broth or fish stock
4 shallots, minced
3 garlic cloves, minced
2 tsps. dried dill weed

1. Mix the potatoes, carrots, mushrooms, shallots, garlic, vegetable broth, and dill weed in a 5.5 litre slow cooker. Cover the slow cooker and cook on low for 6 to 8 hours, or until the vegetables are soft.
2. Place the salmon fillets to the slow cooker. Cover and cook on low for an additional 20 to 30 minutes, or until the salmon flakes when tested with a fork.
3. Gently stir the chowder to break up the salmon.
4. Pour in the milk and Swiss cheese and cover. Let the chowder sit for 10 minutes to let the cheese melt. Stir in the chowder and serve warm.

Nutritional Info per Serving

calories: 453, fat: 20g, protein: 34g, carbs: 31g, fibre: 3g, sugar: 6g, sodium: 252mg

Garlic Roasted Tomato Bisque

SERVES 8-10

| PREP TIME: 12 minutes
| COOK TIME: 9 hours

1.4 kg tomatoes, quartered
2 onions, chopped
2l low-sodium vegetable broth
340ml unsweetened whole milk
2 shallots, minced
4 garlic cloves, minced
1 tsp. dried dill weed
1 tsp. honey
½ tsp. salt
⅛ tsp. freshly ground black pepper

1. Mix the tomatoes, onions, shallots, garlic, and salt in a 5.5 litre slow cooker. Cover the slow cooker and cook on low for 8 hours.
2. Pour the vegetable broth, dill weed, honey, and pepper into the slow cooker. Cover and cook on high for about 50 minutes. Pour in the milk and cook for 10 minutes more.
3. Puree the soup to desired consistency with an immersion blender or a potato masher.

Nutritional Info per Serving

calories: 100, fat: 2g, protein: 4g, carbs: 17g, fibre: 2g, sugar: 10g, sodium: 250mg

Italian Chickpea and Carrot Soup

SERVES 7

| PREP TIME: 20 minutes
| COOK TIME: 6 hours

425 g BPA-free cans no-salt-added chickpeas, drained and rinsed
397 g BPA-free cans diced tomatoes, undrained
4 carrots, peeled and cut into chunks
2 medium parsley roots, peeled and sliced
2 onions, chopped
3 garlic cloves, minced
1.5l low-sodium vegetable broth
1 tsp. dried basil leaves
¼ tsp. freshly ground black pepper

1. Layer all the ingredients in a 5.5 litre slow cooker. Cover the slow cooker and cook on low for 5 to 6 hours, or until the vegetables are soft.
2. Stir in the soup and top with pesto, if desired. Serve warm.

Nutritional Info per Serving

calories: 154, fat: 2g, protein: 6g, carbs: 30g, fibre: 6g, sugar: 10g, sodium: 469mg

Pasta Vegetables Stew

SERVES 6

| PREP TIME: 9 minutes
| COOK TIME: 7½ hours

340g whole-wheat orzo pasta
6 large tomatoes, seeded and chopped
180g sliced cremini mushrooms
180g sliced button mushrooms
300g chopped yellow summer squash
2 red bell peppers, stemmed, seeded, and chopped
2l low-sodium vegetable broth
2 onions, chopped
5 garlic cloves, minced
2 tsps. dried Italian seasoning

1. Mix the onions, garlic, mushrooms, summer squash, bell peppers, tomatoes, vegetable broth, and Italian seasoning in a 5.5 litre slow cooker. Cover the slow cooker and cook on low for 6 to 7 hours, or until the vegetables are soft.
2. Place the pasta and stir. Cover and cook on low for 20 to 30 minutes more, or until the pasta is tender. Enjoy!

Nutritional Info per Serving

calories: 248, fat: 1g, protein: 11g, carbs: 48g, fibre: 9g, sugar: 10g, sodium: 462mg

Curry Yellow Vegetables

SERVES 8

| PREP TIME: 13 minutes
| COOK TIME: 8 hours

4 large carrots, peeled and cut into chunks
2 medium sweet potatoes, peeled and cut into chunks
2 medium courgettes, cut into 2.5cm slices
210g broccoli florets
227 g package button mushrooms, sliced
2 red bell peppers, stemmed, seeded, and chopped
1.2l low-sodium vegetable broth
240ml canned unsweetened coconut milk
2 onions, chopped
3 garlic cloves, minced
2 to 4 tbsps. yellow curry paste

1. Mix all the ingredients in a 5.5 litre slow cooker. Cover the slow cooker and cook on low for 6 to 8 hours, or until the vegetables are soft.
2. Serve hot.

Nutritional Info per Serving

calories: 161, fat: 6g, protein: 4g, carbs: 32g, fibre: 6g, sugar: 9g, sodium: 562mg

Healthy 15-Bean Soup

SERVES 8

| PREP TIME: 11 minutes
| COOK TIME: 6 hours

454 g dried 15-bean mix, rinsed
2.5l low-sodium vegetable broth
3 celery stalks, cut into 1.25cm dice
3 large carrots, cut into 1.25cm dice
1 large onion, cut into 1.25cm dice
1 large bay leaf
1 tbsp. whole-grain mustard

1 tsp. turmeric, ground
1 tsp. kosher salt
½ tsp. no-salt-added poultry seasoning
½ tsp. fennel seed
¼ tsp. black pepper, freshly ground
⅛ tsp. red pepper flakes (optional)

1. In a 7-quart slow cooker, combine the beans, vegetable broth, celery, carrots, onion, bay leaf, mustard, turmeric, salt, poultry seasoning, fennel seed, black pepper, and red pepper flakes, if using. Stir to incorporate well.
2. Cover the cooker. Cook for 4 to 6 hours on high heat or for 8 to 10 hours on low, until the beans are cooked through and very tender. Remove the bay leaf.
3. Portion 340ml of soup each into 4 glass meal-prep containers or pint-size Mason jars with lids. Portion the leftover soup into individual freezer-safe storage containers with lids. Cover, refrigerate, and freeze.

Nutritional Info per Serving

calories: 246, fat: 1.1g, protein: 12g, carbs: 43g, fibre: 18g, sugar: 5g, sodium: 323mg

French Chicken, Mushroom and Wild Rice Stew

SERVES 9

| PREP TIME: 14 minutes
| COOK TIME: 9 hours

10 boneless, skinless chicken thighs, cut into 5cm pieces
397 g BPA-free cans diced tomatoes, undrained
180g sliced cremini mushrooms
3 large carrots, sliced
200g wild rice, rinsed and drained
2 leeks, chopped
90g sliced ripe olives
2l low-sodium vegetable broth
3 garlic cloves, minced
2 tsp. dried herbes de Provence

1. Mix all the ingredients in a 5.5 litre slow cooker. Cover the slow cooker and cook on low for 7 to 9 hours, or until the chicken is cooked to 75°C and the wild rice is soft. Serve warm.

Nutritional Info per Serving

calories: 363, fat: 12g, protein: 32g, carbs: 31g, fibre: 3g, sugar: 5g, sodium: 470mg

Quick Lentil Bisque

SERVES 2-4

| PREP TIME: 2 minutes
| COOK TIME: 20 minutes

200g red lentils, washed and drained
1 white onion, chopped
2 garlic cloves, minced
950ml water

¾ tsp. Himalayan salt
¼ tsp. freshly ground black pepper
1½ tsps. cumin (optional)

1. Combine the lentils, onion, garlic, salt, cumin (if using), and water in a medium stockpot.
2. Bring to a boil, cover, reduce the heat to low and simmer for 20 minutes.
3. Serve right away with freshly ground black pepper, or blend it for a smoother texture.

Nutritional Info per Serving

calories: 370, fat: 2g, protein: 24g, carbs: 67g, fibre: 11g, sugar: 2g, sodium: 358mg

Healthy Veggie Minestrone Soup

SERVES 4

| PREP TIME: 6 minutes
| COOK TIME: 32 minutes

3 tbsps. extra-virgin olive oil
369 g can low-sodium chickpeas, rinsed and drained
2 medium green courgettes, cubed
1 small head broccoli, broken into small, bite-size florets
600g tomato purée (no sugar added)
950ml water
1 large white onion, thinly sliced
1 tsp. Himalayan salt
¾ to 1 tsp. oregano (optional)
¾ to 1 tsp. basil (optional)

1. In a medium stockpot, heat the oil over medium heat.
2. Add the onion and cook for 2 minutes.
3. Place the salt, oregano and basil (if using), followed by the broccoli, courgettes, and chickpeas.
4. Pour in the water and tomato purée. Stir, cover, and cook on low heat for 30 minutes, until the liquid reduces by half and the vegetables are soft.
5. Serve hot.

Nutritional Info per Serving

calories: 313, fat: 13g, protein: 12g, carbs: 42g, fibre: 12g, sugar: 11g, sodium: 576mg

Authentic Ratatouille Soup

SERVES 6

| PREP TIME: 18 minutes
| COOK TIME: 9 hours

2 tbsps. olive oil
6 large tomatoes, seeded and chopped
2 medium aubergines, peeled and chopped
2 red bell peppers, stemmed, seeded, and chopped
340g shredded low-sodium Swiss cheese
1.5l low-sodium vegetable broth
2 onions, chopped
4 garlic cloves, minced
2 tsps. herbes de Provence
2 tbsps. cornflour

1. Mix the olive oil, onions, garlic, aubergines, bell peppers, tomatoes, vegetable broth, and herbes de Provence in a 5.5 litre slow cooker. Cover the slow cooker and cook on low for 7 to 9 hours, or until the vegetables are soft.
2. Toss the cheese with the cornflour in a small bowl. Place the cheese mixture to the slow cooker. Cover and allow to stand for 10 minutes, then stir in the soup and serve warm.

Nutritional Info per Serving

calories: 215, fat: 10g, protein: 9g, carbs: 23g, fibre: 8g, sugar: 11g, sodium: 144mg

CHAPTER 9
APPETIZER AND SIDES

Spicy Mole Chicken Bites / 57

Roasted Coconut Brussels Sprouts / 57

Simple Poached Eggs / 58

Squash Casserole / 58

Bake Potato Fennel / 59

Roasted Beetroot with Rosemary / 59

Grilled Carrots with Dill / 60

Courgette Noodles with Lemon Artichoke

Pesto / 60

Simple Veggie Colcannon / 60

Green Tenderstem broccoli Sauté / 61

Barley Kale Risotto / 61

Spicy Mole Chicken Bites

SERVES 4

| PREP TIME: 10 minutes
| COOK TIME: 6 hours

142 g boneless, skinless chicken breasts
4 large tomatoes, seeded and chopped
1 jalapeño pepper, minced
2 onions, chopped
6 garlic cloves, minced
2 dried red chillies, crushed
120ml low-sodium chicken stock
3 tbsps. cocoa powder
2 tbsps. chilli powder
2 tbsps. coconut sugar

1. Mix the onions, garlic, tomatoes, chilli peppers, and jalapeño peppers in a 5.5 litre slow cooker.
2. In a medium bowl, mix the cocoa powder, chilli powder, coconut sugar, and chicken stock.
3. Slice the chicken breasts into 2.5cm strips crosswise and place to the slow cooker. Add the chicken stock mixture over all.
4. Cover the slow cooker and cook on low for 4 to 6 hours, or until the chicken registers 75°C on a food thermometer. Serve warm with toothpicks or little plates and forks.

Nutritional Info per Serving

calories: 157, fat: 3g, protein: 23g, carbs: 12g, fibre: 2g, sugar: 8g, sodium: 249mg

Roasted Coconut Brussels Sprouts

SERVES 4

| PREP TIME: 12 minutes
| COOK TIME: 30 minutes

907 g Brussels sprouts, trimmed and cut in half
2 tsps. coconut oil, melted
15g unsweetened toasted desiccated coconut

1. Preheat the oven to 205°C. Line a baking sheet with foil.
2. In a large bowl, toss the Brussels sprouts with the melted coconut oil until the vegetables are well coated.
3. Spread the Brussels sprouts on the prepared baking sheet in one layer and roast until they are tender and browned, about 20 to 30 minutes.
4. Serve topped with toasted coconut.

calories: 117, fat: 3g, protein: 8g, carbs: 21g, fibre: 9g, sugar: 5g, sodium: 57mg

Nutritional Info per Serving

Simple Poached Eggs

SERVES 1

| PREP TIME: 2 minutes
| COOK TIME: 5 minutes

1.5l water
A pinch of salt
1 tsp. vinegar
2 large eggs

1. Add the salt and the vinegar to a medium saucepan with water and bring it to a boil over high heat.
2. Crack each egg in its own small bowl.
3. When reaching a boil, turn down the heat until it comes to a slow and steady simmer.
4. Swirl the water in a circle with a spoon to create a vortex and slide the egg(s) into water.
5. Cook for 4 minutes and then remove the eggs with a slotted spoon.
6. If you prefer your yolks on the runnier side, cook for 3 minutes. If you prefer them hard, cook longer, for 5 to 6 minutes.

Nutritional Info per Serving

calories: 152, fat: 9g, protein: 12g, carbs: 0.8g, fibre: 0g, sugar: 0.2g, sodium: 298mg

Squash Casserole

SERVES 8

| PREP TIME: 5 minutes
| COOK TIME: 1 hour

Nonstick cooking spray
1 large butternut squash, cut in half and seeded
120ml canned unsweetened low-fat coconut milk
2 eggs
2 tbsps. pure maple syrup
4 tsps. cornflour
1 tsp. cinnamon, ground
¼ tsp. nutmeg, ground
¼ tsp. cloves, ground

1. Preheat the oven to 205ºC. Line a baking sheet with foil and lightly coat the foil with cooking spray.
2. Place the squash cut-side down on the baking sheet and bake until tender and collapsed, about 30 minutes.
3. Remove the squash from the oven and cool for about 10 minutes.
4. Reduce the oven temperature to 180ºC.
5. Use a spoon to scoop out the flesh of the squash.
6. In a food processor or blender, process the squash with the remaining ingredients until smooth, scraping down the sides of the bowl at least once.
7. Spoon the squash mixture into a casserole and bake, for about 30 minutes until the mixture is set.
8. Serve warm.

Nutritional Info per Serving

calories: 132, fat: 5g, protein: 3g, carbs: 22g, fibre: 4g, sugar: 9g, sodium: 25mg

Bake Potato Fennel

SERVES 4

| PREP TIME: 15 minutes
| COOK TIME: 50 minutes

2 large Yukon gold potatoes, skin on, washed and thinly sliced
1 tbsp. olive oil
Black pepper, freshly ground
1 medium fennel bulb, trimmed and thinly sliced
2 tsps. fresh thyme, chopped
2 garlic cloves, thinly sliced
Zest and juice of 1 lemon
240ml low-sodium, fat-free vegetable stock

1. Preheat the oven to 180°C.
2. Toss the potatoes with the oil in a medium bowl. Season lightly with the pepper.
3. In a 23 by 28cm baking dish, make an even layer of half the fennel slices.
4. Place half the potatoes, half the thyme, and half the garlic on the top the fennel.
5. Repeat the layering to use up all the fennel, potatoes, thyme, and garlic.
6. Sprinkle with lemon zest and juice.
7. Pour in the vegetable stock and cover with foil.
8. Bake until very tender, about 45 minutes.
9. Remove the foil and bake for 5 more minutes to brown the potatoes.
10. Serve immediately.

Nutritional Info per Serving

calories: 168, fat: 4g, protein: 4g, carbs: 34g, fibre: 6g, sugar: 2g, sodium: 81mg

Roasted Beetroot with Rosemary

SERVES 4

| PREP TIME: 9 minutes
| COOK TIME: 35 minutes

700g beetroot, peeled and quartered
1 tbsp. olive oil
1 tbsp. fresh rosemary, chopped
Pinch of sea salt

1. Preheat the oven to 205°C. Line a baking tray with foil.
2. In a large bowl, toss the beetroot with the oil to coat the beetroot.
3. Spread the beetroot on the prepared baking sheet and roast in the oven until tender and lightly browned, about 25 to 35 minutes.
4. Remove the beetroot from the oven. Sprinkle with the rosemary.
5. Season with salt and serve hot.

Nutritional Info per Serving

calories: 91, fat: 4g, protein: 2g, carbs: 15g, fibre: 4g, sugar: 9g, sodium: 165mg

Grilled Carrots with Dill

SERVES 4

| PREP TIME: 6 minutes
| COOK TIME: 10 minutes

454 g carrots, washed and cut into batons
1 tsp. olive oil

1 tbsp. fresh dill, chopped
1 tbsp. fresh lemon juice

1. Preheat the barbecue to medium-high heat or preheat the broiler.
2. On the barbecue, grill the carrots until softened and lightly charred, turning frequently, about 10 minutes. Or in the oven, broil the carrots, turning once, until tender, about 8 minutes.
3. In a large bowl, combine the carrots with the remaining ingredients and toss.
4. Serve warm.

Nutritional Info per Serving

calories: 59, fat: 2g, protein: 1g, carbs: 11g, fibre: 4g, sugar: 6g, sodium: 80mg

Courgette Noodles with Lemon Artichoke Pesto

SERVES 4

| PREP TIME: 26 minutes
| COOK TIME: 0 minutes

170g artichoke hearts, chopped
10g packed fresh basil leaves
65g pecan halves, chopped
2 tsps. garlic, minced
Zest and juice of 1 lemon

Pinch of black pepper, freshly ground
60ml olive oil
2 large courgettes, julienned
400g cherry tomatoes, halved
Pinch of red pepper flakes, crushed

1. In a food processor or blender, add half the artichoke hearts with the basil, pecans, garlic, lemon zest, lemon juice, and black pepper. Pulse until very finely chopped.
2. Add the olive oil and pulse until blended.
3. In a large bowl, toss the courgette "noodles" with the remaining artichoke hearts, cherry tomatoes, and red pepper flakes until well mixed.
4. Add the pesto by tablespoons until it reaches the desired flavour and texture.
5. Store any leftover pesto in a sealed container in the fridge for up to 2 weeks.
6. Serve immediately.

Nutritional Info per Serving

calories: 259, fat: 23g, protein: 5g, carbs: 14g, fibre: 5g, sugar: 5g, sodium: 106mg

Simple Veggie Colcannon

SERVES 4

| PREP TIME: 9 minutes
| COOK TIME: 25 minutes

6 large russet potatoes, peeled and chopped into 1.25cm chunks
1 tsp. olive oil
1 small sweet onion, peeled and diced

3 tsps. garlic, minced
400g kale, chopped
240ml unsweetened almond milk
Pinch of sea salt
Pinch of black pepper, freshly ground

1. Bring a large pot of water to a boil over medium-high heat.
2. Add the potatoes and boil until tender, about 15 minutes.
3. Drain and rinse the potatoes, and transfer them to a large bowl.
4. In a large frying pan over medium-high heat, heat the oil and sauté the onion and garlic for 3 minutes or until softened.
5. Add the kale and sauté until wilted, about 3 minutes.
6. Mash the potatoes with the almond milk, salt, and pepper until smooth.
7. Add the kale mixture to the mashed potatoes and stir until well combined.
8. Serve warm.

Nutritional Info per Serving

calories: 370, fat: 2g, protein: 11g, carbs: 77g, fibre: 9g, sugar: 4g, sodium: 189mg

Green Tenderstem broccoli Sauté

SERVES 4

| PREP TIME: 8 minutes
| COOK TIME: 10 minutes

3 tsps. olive oil
700g tenderstem broccoli, chopped (about 3 bunches)
3 spring onions, chopped
4 roasted garlic cloves, sliced or chopped
½ tsp. black pepper, freshly ground
¼ tsp. red pepper flakes, crushed
90g baby spinach
5g fresh parsley, chopped
Zest and juice of 1 lemon

1. In a large frying pan over medium heat, heat the oil and sauté the tenderstem broccoli, spring onions, and roasted garlic until the tenderstem broccoli is bright green but still crisp, about 5 minutes.
2. Add the black pepper and red pepper flakes and stir to combine.
3. Add the spinach, parsley, and lemon zest and sauté until the spinach is wilted, about 3 minutes.
4. Add the lemon juice to the frying pan and stir.
5. Serve immediately.

Nutritional Info per Serving

calories: 81, fat: 4g, protein: 4g, carbs: 8g, fibre: 2g, sugar: 3g, sodium: 47mg

Barley Kale Risotto

SERVES 4

| PREP TIME: 8 minutes
| COOK TIME: 1 hour

1 medium butternut squash, peeled, seeded, and cut into 1.25cm cubes
2 tsps. olive oil, divided
Pinch of black pepper, freshly ground
½ small sweet onion, peeled and finely chopped
1 tsp. garlic, minced
170g barley, hulled and rinsed
400g kale, chopped
2 tbsps. pine nuts
2 tbsps. fresh thyme, chopped

1. Preheat the oven to 190ºC. Line a baking sheet with foil.
2. Toss the squash with 1 tsp. of the oil and the pepper.
3. Spread the squash on the baking sheet and roast in the oven until the squash is tender and lightly browned, stirring several times, about 35 minutes.
4. While the squash is roasting, fill a medium saucepan with about 1.2l of water and bring to a boil.
5. Lower the heat to keep the water warm but not simmering.
6. In a large saucepan over medium heat, add the remaining tsp. of oil. Sauté the onion and garlic in the oil until softened, about 3 minutes.
7. Add the barley and sauté, stirring, for about 2 minutes.
8. Add one cup of the hot water to the barley. Stir until the water is absorbed.
9. Repeat until you have added 700ml of hot water to the barley.
10. Add the kale and stir until the kale is wilted and the water is absorbed.
11. Add more water, a small amount at a time, stirring often, until the barley is cooked through and tender.
12. Stir in the roasted squash and the pine nuts.
13. Serve the risotto topped with thyme.

Nutritional Info per Serving

calories: 323, fat: 8g, protein: 10g, carbs: 59g, fibre: 10g, sugar: 6g, sodium: 37mg

CHAPTER 10

SNACK AND DESSERT

Chocolate and Coconut Oat Bites / 63

Cheese and Bean-Stuffed Mini Sweet Peppers / 63

Sweet and Spicy Mixed Nuts / 64

Almond Banana Mini Muffins / 64

Strawberry Lemonade Slushie / 65

Sweet Potato and Tomato Bites / 65

Tasty Edamame / 66

Tropical Pineapple Fruit Leather / 66

Chilli-Spiced Fruit Cups / 66

Buffalo Cauliflower Bites / 67

Grilled Peaches with Maple Walnuts / 67

Chocolate and Coconut Oat Bites

SERVES 12

| PREP TIME: 25 minutes
| COOK TIME: 0 minutes

115g gluten-free oats
185g seed butter, such as sunflower
30g cup ground flaxseed
15g shredded coconut
57 g unsweetened mini dark chocolate chips
1 tbsp. honey
2 tsps. chia seeds
1 tsp. vanilla extract
1 tsp. sea salt

1. Combine all the ingredients in a bowl. Put the bowl in the refrigerator for about 25 minutes to set.
2. Shape the dough into 2.5cm balls and enjoy.

Nutritional Info per Serving
calories: 185, fat: 13g, protein: 5g, carbs: 14g, fibre: 3g, sugar: 4g, sodium: 208mg

Cheese and Bean-Stuffed Mini Sweet Peppers

SERVES 6

| PREP TIME: 5 minutes
| COOK TIME: 23 minutes

40g ground lupin bean
6 mini sweet peppers, cut in half lengthwise
57 g low-fat goat cheese, crumbled
2 tbsps. chopped spring onions
1 tsp. garlic powder

1. Preheat the oven to 205°C and line a sheet pan with unbleached parchment paper.
2. In a microwave-safe dish, combine the ground lupin bean and ¼ cup of water. Microwave for about 3 minutes on High. Put the garlic powder and goat cheese and mix well.
3. Place the peppers cut-side up on the sheet pan. Spoon the ground lupin mixture evenly into each pepper. Bake for about 20 minutes.
4. Put the stuffed peppers on a platter and garnish with the spring onions. Serve warm.

Nutritional Info per Serving
calories: 66, fat: 3g, protein: 5g, carbs: 5g, fibre: 3g, sugar: 0g, sodium: 44mg

Sweet and Spicy Mixed Nuts

SERVES 12

| PREP TIME: 5 minutes
| COOK TIME: 15 minutes

2 tbsps. avocado oil
450g raw unsalted mixed nuts
2 tbsps. 100% pure maple syrup
1 tsp. vanilla extract
¼ tsp. sea salt
¼ tsp. ground cumin
⅛ tsp. cayenne pepper

1. Preheat the oven to 165ºC and line a sheet pan with unbleached parchment paper.
2. Combine all the ingredients well in a large bowl.
3. Spread the nut mixture evenly on the sheet pan and bake for about 15 minutes. Enjoy!

Nutritional Info per Serving

calories: 200, fat: 17g, protein: 5g, carbs: 8g, fibre: 2g, sugar: 3g, sodium: 49mg

Almond Banana Mini Muffins

SERVES 24

| PREP TIME: 3 minutes
| COOK TIME: 12 minutes

3 tbsps. avocado oil
240g almond flour
155g chopped pistachios, divided
2 large eggs
2 bananas, mashed
120 unsweetened coconut yoghurt

1 tsp. vanilla extract
1 tsp. baking soda
½ tsp. almond extract
½ tsp. baking powder
¼ tsp. sea salt

1. Preheat the oven to 400° F and grease a 24-well mini muffin pan lightly with non stick avocado oil cooking spray.
2. Sift together the almond flour, baking soda, baking powder, and salt in a small bowl.
3. In a separate large bowl, beat the eggs, then add the avocado oil, coconut yoghurt, mashed bananas, vanilla extract, and almond extract. Mix well.
4. Place the dry mixture gradually to the egg and banana mixture, stirring constantly.
5. Slowly fold in ¾ cup of chopped pistachios.
6. Scoop the batter into the muffin pan, filling each well about ⅔ full. Scatter the remaining ½ cup of pistachios evenly over the muffins.
7. Bake for about 10 to 12 minutes, or until a toothpick comes out clean. Serve hot.

Nutritional Info per Serving

calories: 130, fat: 10g, protein: 5g, carbs: 6g, fibre: 2g, sugar: 2g, sodium: 71mg

Strawberry Lemonade Slushie

SERVES 4

| PREP TIME: 4 minutes
| COOK TIME: 0 minutes

454 g frozen strawberries
240ml water
14 ice cubes (1 tray) ice
Juice of 3 lemons
1 tbsp. honey

1. Put all of the ingredients in a blender. Pulse on high until smooth.
2. Pour into four glasses. Decorate with fresh strawberry and lemon slices.
3. Serve immediately.

Nutritional Info per Serving
calories: 65, fat: 0.2g, protein: 0.6g, carbs: 17g, fibre: 1.7g, sugar: 9g, sodium: 3mg

Sweet Potato and Tomato Bites

SERVES 4

| PREP TIME: 7 minutes
| COOK TIME: 20 minutes

1 tbsp. olive oil
3 medium sweet potatoes, cut into 6.5mm slices
1 tomato, cut into 6.5mm dice
1 avocado, diced
45g frozen roasted corn, thawed
55g canned black beans
½ red onion, cut into 6.5mm dice
Juice of 1 lime
3 tbsps. chopped coriander
½ tsp. cumin
¼ tsp. garlic powder
¼ tsp. sea salt

1. Preheat the oven to 200ºC and line a sheet pan with unbleached parchment paper.
2. Arrange the sweet potato slices on the sheet pan and bake them for about 20 minutes.
3. When the sweet potatoes are baking, mix the avocado, roasted corn, black beans, onion, tomato, olive oil, garlic powder, cumin, salt, and lime juice in a large bowl.
4. Pour the avocado mixture over the sweet potato slices and serve on a platter.

Nutritional Info per Serving
calories: 217, fat: 9g, protein: 4g, carbs: 32g, fibre: 8g, sugar: 6g, sodium: 206mg

Tasty Edamame

SERVES 4

PREP TIME: 4 minutes	1 tbsp. sesame oil	2 tsps. chilli paste
COOK TIME: 9 minutes	454 g edamame in pods	1 tsp. tamari
	2 garlic cloves, minced	¼ tsp. kosher salt

1. Bring a medium saucepan of water to a boil. Place the edamame and cook for about 4 minutes. Drain well.
2. When the edamame cooks, heat the sesame oil in a separate sauté pan over medium heat. Place the garlic and chilli paste. Heat until fragrant, then put the drained edamame and tamari. Stir to combine well.
3. Serve the edamame in a large bowl and sprinkle with the kosher salt.

Nutritional Info per Serving

calories: 188, fat: 8g, protein: 16g, carbs: 15g, fibre: 5g, sugar: 2g, sodium: 293mg

Tropical Pineapple Fruit Leather

SERVES 6

PREP TIME: 6 minutes	1 pineapple, cored and chopped
COOK TIME: 4-5 hours	1 mango, peeled and chopped
	1 tbsp. honey
	Juice and zest of 1 lemon

1. Preheat the oven to 95ºC. Line a baking sheet with a silicone baking mat or parchment paper.
2. Blend all of the ingredients into on high until smooth.
3. Transfer the mixture onto the baking sheet. Evenly spread it out in a layer. Bake for 4 to 5 hours or until a inserted toothpick comes out clean.
4. Cool completely, cut into strips and roll up in parchment paper.
5. Serve immediately.

Nutritional Info per Serving

calories: 78, fat: 0.3g, protein: 0.2g, carbs: 18g, fibre: 2.5g, sugar: 15g, sodium: 6mg

Chilli-Spiced Fruit Cups

SERVES 8

PREP TIME: 7 minutes	1 pineapple
COOK TIME: 0 minutes	2 mangoes
	1 small seedless watermelon
	1 cucumber
	Juice of 1 lime
	1 tsp. chilli powder
	½ tsp. salt

1. Chop the fruits listed above to equal-size cubes.
2. Place the fruit and cucumber cubes into a large bowl. Toss with the lime juice, chilli powder, and season with salt.
3. Serve immediately.

Nutritional Info per Serving

calories: 118, fat: 0.3g, protein: 3g, carbs: 28g, fibre: 4g, sugar: 24g, sodium: 154mg

Buffalo Cauliflower Bites

SERVES 4

| PREP TIME: 10 minutes
| COOK TIME: 22 minutes

1 large cauliflower head, cut into bite-size florets
120ml unsweetened almond milk
60g almond flour
1 bunch spring onions, chopped
2 tbsps. tamari
2 tbsps. honey
1 tbsp. apple cider vinegar
1 tbsp. paprika
1½ tsps. garlic powder, divided
¼ tsp. sea salt
⅛ tsp. cayenne pepper

1. Preheat the oven to 200ºC and line a sheet pan with unbleached parchment paper.
2. Mix together the almond flour, almond milk, ½ tsp. garlic powder, and salt in a small bowl. Place the cauliflower to the bowl and toss in the batter to coat well.
3. Evenly spread the cauliflower onto the sheet pan and bake for about 6 minutes. Gently flip the cauliflower and bake for an additional 6 minutes.
4. When the cauliflower is baking, combine the apple cider vinegar, tamari, honey, paprika, remaining 1 tsp. garlic powder, and cayenne pepper in a separate bowl.
5. Coat the cauliflower with the sauce and take back to the oven to cook for 10 minutes more.
6. Serve the cauliflower bites on a platter, garnished with the spring onions.

Nutritional Info per Serving
calories: 192, fat: 8g, protein: 9g, carbs: 26g, fibre: 7g, sugar: 12g, sodium: 741mg

Grilled Peaches with Maple Walnuts

SERVES 4

| PREP TIME: 4 minutes
| COOK TIME: 8 minutes

1 tbsp. avocado oil
4 ripe peaches, halved and pitted
40g chopped walnuts
8 mint leaves
2 tbsps. 100% pure maple syrup
½ tsp. vanilla extract
⅛ tsp. kosher salt

1. Heat a grill or grill pan on the stovetop to medium-high heat. Coat the peaches with the avocado oil and arrange them on the grill cut-side down. Cook for about 4 minutes, then flip skin-side down and grill for an additional 4 minutes.
2. When the peaches are grilling, add the walnuts, vanilla, salt, and maple syrup to a sauté pan over medium heat. Heat them until fragrant, gently adding up to 3 tbsps. of water if the walnuts start to stick.
3. Put the peaches on a plate, add the walnut mixture over the top, sprinkle with the mint, and serve warm.

Nutritional Info per Serving
calories: 164, fat: 9g, protein: 3g, carbs: 22g, fibre: 3g, sugar: 18g, sodium: 40mg

APPENDIX 1: 30 DAYS MEAL PLAN

Meal Plan	Breakfast	Lunch	Dinner	Snack/Dessert
Day-1	Potato, Tomato and Egg Strata	Vegetables and Grains	Pork Chops and Carrot	Buffalo Cauliflower Bites
Day-2	Cinnamon Apple French Toast Bake	Roasted Beet, Kale and Quinoa	BBQ Pulled Pork	Chocolate and Coconut Oat Bites
Day-3	Kale and Quinoa Egg Casserole	Barley Risotto with Mushroom	Apples-Onions Pork Chops	Cheese and Bean-Stuffed Mini Sweet Peppers
Day-4	Apple-Cranberry Quinoa	Cheesy Risotto with Green Beans and Sweet Potatoes	Bean Tostadas	Sweet and Spicy Mixed Nuts
Day-5	Savoury Spinach Oatmeal	Garlicky Tofu and Brussels Sprouts	Roasted Sweet Potato, Carrot and Quinoa Salad	Grilled Peaches with Maple Walnuts
Day-6	Mixed Nuts Berry Granola	Garlic Barley and Black Beans	Vegetable Chilli	Almond Banana Mini Muffins
Day-7	Mediterranean Spinach Strata	Rosemary White Beans with Onion	Shakshuka with Red Peppers	Tasty Edamame
Day-8	Garlic Root Vegetable Hash	Thai Green Bean and Soybean	Cauliflower and Cashew Gratin	Tropical Pineapple Fruit Leather
Day-9	Grain Granola with Dry Cherries	Herbed Succotash with Tomato	Healthy Mushroom Cashew Rice	Chilli-Spiced Fruit Cups
Day-10	Baked Berries Oatmeal	Beef and Mushroom Lo Mein	Tandoori Courgette Cauliflower Curry	Sweet Potato and Tomato Bites

Meal Plan	Breakfast	Lunch	Dinner	Snack/Dessert
Day-11	Kale and Quinoa Egg Casserole	Sweet Pepper with Sirloin	Balsamic Chicken Caprese Bowl	Lemon Avocado Tuna Salad
Day-12	Savoury Spinach Oatmeal	Classic Moroccan Beef in Lettuce Cups	Sheet-Pan Chicken Fajitas	Curry Yellow Vegetables
Day-13	Spicy Eggs in Purgatory	Mustard Beef Brisket	Chicken Marinara Meatballs	Strawberry Lemonade Slushie
Day-14	Quinoa with Mushroom and Carrot	Cheesy Risotto with Green Beans and Sweet Potatoes	Spicy Black Bean, Sweet Potato and Brown Rice Sliders	Green Tenderstem broccoli Sauté
Day-15	Wild Rice with Parsley	Beef Tenderloin with Onion Marmalade	Roasted Sweet Potato, Carrot and Quinoa Salad	Cheese and Bean-Stuffed Mini Sweet Peppers
Day-16	Potato, Tomato and Egg Strata	Moroccan Beef Tagine	BBQ Pulled Pork	Chocolate and Coconut Oat Bites
Day-17	Grain Granola with Dry Cherries	Vegetables and Grains	Bean Tostadas	Buffalo Cauliflower Bites
Day-18	Mixed Nuts Berry Granola	Classic Lamb and Aubergine Tikka Masala	Red Lentil and Coconut Curry	Grilled Peaches with Maple Walnuts
Day-19	Apple-Cranberry Quinoa	Barley Risotto with Mushroom	Healthy Mushroom Cashew Rice	Sweet and Spicy Mixed Nuts
Day-20	Cinnamon Apple French Toast Bake	Beef and Mushroom Lo Mein	Turmeric Sweet Potato Soup	Quick Lentil Bisque

Meal Plan	Breakfast	Lunch	Dinner	Snack/Dessert
Day-21	Baked Berries Oatmeal	Rosemary White Beans with Onion	Apples-Onions Pork Chops	Bake Potato Fennel
Day-22	Grain Granola with Dry Cherries	Beef Tenderloin with Onion Marmalade	Spicy Black Bean, Sweet Potato and Brown Rice Sliders	Roasted Beetroot with Rosemary
Day-23	Kale and Quinoa Egg Casserole	Sweet Pepper with Sirloin	Red Lentil and Coconut Curry	Chilli-Spiced Fruit Cups
Day-24	Mediterranean Spinach Strata	Beef and Mushroom Lo Mein	Pork Chops and Carrot	Strawberry Lemonade Slushie
Day-25	Cinnamon Apple French Toast Bake	Herbed Succotash with Tomato	Vegetables Chickpea Curry	Almond Banana Mini Muffins
Day-26	Garlic Root Vegetable Hash	Thai Green Bean and Soybean	Cauliflower and Cashew Gratin	Grilled Peaches with Maple Walnuts
Day-27	Mixed Nuts Berry Granola	Garlic Barley and Black Beans	Vegetable Chilli	Sweet and Spicy Mixed Nuts
Day-28	Savoury Spinach Oatmeal	Garlicky Tofu and Brussels Sprouts	Shakshuka with Red Peppers	Cheese and Bean-Stuffed Mini Sweet Peppers
Day-29	Apple-Cranberry Quinoa	Roasted Beet, Kale and Quinoa	BBQ Pulled Pork	Chocolate and Coconut Oat Bites
Day-30	Potato, Tomato and Egg Strata	Vegetables and Grains	Apples-Onions Pork Chops	Buffalo Cauliflower Bites

A

ACORN SQUASH

Baked Acorn Squash and Rocket Salad 42

APPLE

Cinnamon Apple French Toast Bake 9

AUBERGINE

Authentic Ratatouille Soup 55

AVOCADO

Cherry Tomato and Avocado Salad 39

Rocket Watermelon and Avocado Salad 41

B

BANANA

Almond Banana Mini Muffins 64

BEEF BRISKET

Mustard Beef Brisket 22

BEEF SIRLOIN

Classic Moroccan Beef in Lettuce Cups 24

Moroccan Beef Tagine 21

BEEF TENDERLOIN

Beef Tenderloin with Onion Marmalade 25

BEETROOT

Roasted Beet and Pistachio Salad 39

Roasted Beetroot with Rosemary 59

BLACK BEAN

Bean Tostadas 30

Garlic Barley and Black Beans 16

BLUEBERRY

Baked Berries Oatmeal 11

Mixed Nuts Berry Granola 11

BROCCOLI

Creamy Broccoli and Cauliflower Soup 51

Green Tenderstem broccoli Sauté 61

Vegetables and Grains 19

BRUSSELS SPROUT

Garlicky Tofu and Brussels Sprouts 19

Roasted Coconut Brussels Sprouts 57

BUTTERNUT SQUASH

Squash Casserole 58

BUTTON MUSHROOM

Barley Risotto with Mushroom 16

Healthy Mushroom Cashew Rice 28

C

CARROT

Curry Yellow Vegetables 53

Grilled Carrots with Dill 60

CAULIFLOWER

Buffalo Cauliflower Bites 67

Cauliflower and Cashew Gratin

CHICKEN

Chicken Enchiladas 34

Chicken Marinara Meatballs 33

CHICKEN BREAST

Balsamic Chicken Caprese Bowl 36

Chicken with Squash and Mushroom 37

Delicious Chicken Marsala 37

Peachy Chicken Picante 35

Savoury Chicken Bruschetta Pasta 36

Sheet-Pan Chicken Fajitas 33

Spicy Mole Chicken Bites 57

CHICKEN THIGH

French Chicken, Mushroom and Wild Rice
Stew 54

Jerk Chicken Thigh 34

Oven Chicken Thighs with Paprika 35

CHICKPEA

Italian Chickpea and Carrot Soup 52

Vegetables Chickpea Curry 29

COURGETTE

Courgette Noodles with Lemon Artichoke
Pesto 60

Tandoori Courgette Cauliflower Curry 30

CRANBERRY

Apple-Cranberry Quinoa 10

CREMINI MUSHROOM

Pasta Vegetables Stew 53

Quinoa with Mushroom and Carrot 18
CUCUMBER
Chickpea Salad with Olives and Cucumber 43

E-K

EDAMAME
Tasty Edamame 66
GREEN BEAN
Thai Green Bean and Soybean 18
KALE
Barley Kale Risotto 61
Kale and Quinoa Egg Casserole 9
Roasted Beet, Kale and Quinoa 15

L

LAMB
Classic Lamb and Aubergine Tikka Masala 24
Feta Lamb Burgers 24
LENTIL
Quick Lentil Bisque 54
Red Lentil and Coconut Curry 27
LIMA BEAN
Herbed Succotash with Tomato 17
LUPIN BEAN
Cheese and Bean-Stuffed Mini Sweet
Peppers 63

M

MAHI-MAHI
Crispy Mahi-Mahi Tenders 49
MANGO
Flavourful Mango and Bean Salad 42

P

PEACH
Grilled Peaches with Maple Walnuts 67
PINEAPPLE
Chilli-Spiced Fruit Cups 66

Tropical Pineapple Fruit Leather 66
PORK CHOP
Apples-Onions Pork Chops 23
Pork Chops and Carrot 22
PORK SHOULDER
BBQ Pulled Pork 23

R

RED PEPPER
Shakshuka with Red Peppers 31

S

SALMON
Baked Salmon and Asparagus 46
Maple Cedar Plank Salmon 45
Parmesan Salmon with Root Vegetables 48
Salmon and Veggies Ratatouille 47
Salmon Vegetables Chowder 51
Salmon, Mushroom and Barley Bake 49
SHRIMP
Mushroom Shrimp Scampi 45
SPINACH
Caprese Salad Quinoa Bowl 42
Mediterranean Spinach Strata 13
Savoury Spinach Oatmeal 10
STRAWBERRY
Strawberry Lemonade Slushie 65
SWEET POTATO
Cheesy Risotto with Green Beans and
Sweet Potatoes 18
Roasted Sweet Potato, Carrot and Quinoa
Salad 27
Spicy Black Bean, Sweet Potato and Brown
Rice Sliders 30
Sweet Potato and Tomato Bites 65
Turmeric Sweet Potato Soup 29

T

TOMATO
Garlic Roasted Tomato Bisque 52

Greek Cherry Tomato Quinoa Salad   41
Potato, Tomato and Egg Strata   13
TOP SIRLOIN STEAK
Sweet Pepper with Sirloin   21
TUNA
Lemon Avocado Tuna Salad   40
Quick Grilled Ahi Tuna   48
Tuna and Carrot Salad   47
Tuna and Spinach Burgers   48

W

WHITE BEAN
Rosemary White Beans with Onion   17
WHITE FISH
White Fish and Spinach Risotto   46

Y

YUKON GOLD POTATO
Bake Potato Fennel   59
Garlic Root Vegetable Hash   12

Printed in Great Britain
by Amazon

37419391R00044